LIVING WITH PURPOSE AND POWER

Create Your Guiding Stars and Live Your Ultimate Life

KELLAN FLUCKIGER

Living With Purpose and Power
Create Your Guiding Stars and Live Your Ultimate Life

Contact the Publisher:

Joy Fluckiger, CEO Red Aussie Publishing
redaussiepublishing@gmail.com
www.kellanfluckiger.com

Printed in the United States of America
First Edition 2024

Cover Art: Joy Fluckiger

ISBN: 978-1-990090-15-8

RED AUSSIE
PUBLISHING

LIVING WITH PURPOSE AND POWER

Table of Contents

Foreword

We all want to be happy. We all want to make a difference for good. The question always seems to be how best to do that. We are so busy surviving and dealing with life's challenges that most of our noble desires end up taking a back seat to the noise of everyday living, the intense barrage of bad news, and left-over whispers of doubt from the past.

At the same time, we have a yearning. A sense deep within us that there is more to life than the obvious. We are designed to matter; we yearn to love and be loved. We are happiest when we are in service to those around us, and all about adding good to the world.

The powerful truth about you and your life is you need no one's permission to be your best self. You need no one's agreement to love and serve. You must only declare to yourself and your creator who you are and live into that declaration with all your soul. I have dedicated my life to helping people see who they really are and create from that infinite possibility.

I met Kellan about six years ago when I spoke at a mastermind of one of my clients. Since then, I have read many of his books, had dinner with him at my house, and had the chance to peer deep into his soul. I love what I see. Kellan is a man who has walked through the valley of the shadow of death and chosen to come out with a light and a power I have rarely seen.

Every person has exquisitely tailored events that test their being and prove their mettle. Those events either ruin us or they refine us. Sometimes both. Our ultimate opportunity and power are to choose who we are and what each of those circumstances brings forward from our inner selves.

In this book, Kellan has poured everything he has learned and personally experienced in the crucible of his experience. It is a guide to create your own purpose and power, if you choose it. As with all powerful books about growth and choice, the stories are not about the author, though they come from his life. They are signposts to illustrate what is possible for you.

You can wander around all your life wondering what you should do and how to find your mission and purpose. Or you can follow the yearning of your deepest heart and dive into the processes and directions of this book. You can choose to create an awesome masterpiece with your life that shines as a light to bless those you meet and serve those you can.

I love the ideas, principles, and instructions in this book. I love the man who wrote this book. I invite you to do what I do and use the principles and practices of this book to create your own life of purpose and power fueled by pure love and founded on service.

Magic and infinite joy await those who dare.

Loving You. Be Blessed. SFH/kab

Steve Hardison

Mesa Arizona

August 2023

Introduction

This book will change your life.

Or it will do nothing.

Your choice.

People talk all the time about finding a life purpose. Most never really feel they have a handle on what that is. It seems to be an imaginary state where, every day, you know who you are, what you are about, what to do, and feel excitedly engaged in your purpose.

Perhaps, like you, I never knew what my purpose was. I had some vague ideas about what I was "supposed to do," but no big purpose that created any fire in the belly.

So, I lived pursuing the golden ticket of money, position, and being "important." That path led me through the nightmare of multiple failed relationships, addictions, and attempted suicide. The story of that journey of personal terror is in *Tightrope of Depression – My Journey from Darkness, Despair, and Death to Light, Love, and Life.*

We all want to matter and have a big impact. We all want to have abundance. We deeply desire to love and be loved. We seek experiences we remember and treasure. We want deep and meaningful relationships. With all this wanting, most don't really take the yearning to ground and create the life they desire.

What's missing is the creation element. We avoid the work and assume things will "happen to us" so the path will be clear. It doesn't work that way. We must choose, work, evaluate, and choose again.

We live in a world where most would rather watch and wish. This book is written to help you choose to turn your thoughts into things and your inner yearning into your wonderful truth.

When my transformation journey started in August 2007, I would not have predicted writing this book. In fact, I had no intention of writing any book. I had barely begun a journey of sobriety after ending a $3000/week drug habit in a single day. At the same time, I walked away from a 30-year career while at the top of my game because it was killing me.

I hated myself, everything I was doing, and the multifaced person I was being. The story of the miraculous divine intervention and invitation that saved my life and my soul is in *Tightrope of Depression,* chapters 60 – 68.

Until that moment, I lived a horrifying rollercoaster of illusion, misery, and self-sabotage in the fearful grip of the heartless monsters of depression, self-loathing, and self-sabotage.

From 2008 to 2018, I experienced a ten-year journey of discovery, recovery, and growth aimed at finding out who I really was and what I was meant to do. It was a complicated and sometimes confusing process that consumed every bit of the ten years. That story is in *Down from the Gallows – The Myth, The Truth and Battles of a Creative with Depression.*

I am writing this book for three reasons. First, beginning with the miracles of August 2007, my life changed in powerful and joyful ways. I could never have imagined the radical shifts that would bring me to who I am and how much I love life every single minute. Even at the conclusion of *Down from the Gallows* in 2018, I could not have foreseen the awesome opportunity and the amazing trajectory life has taken since that time.

The radical shifts came as I learned and applied truths that came to me along a difficult, dangerous, enlightening, and unexpected journey. Creation is not random but follows the application of the principles that govern the process.

Second, I must share the pure gold I discovered as I was guided and helped along this path. The truths I share are not original. I did not invent truth. Truth is eternal and stands outside my ability to create or destroy. I now understood and can take full advantage of truths that govern creation, love, service, joy and other eternal principles.

This book is not about me, though I am in the stories. The stories are to illustrate points I learned and want to share with you. However, if you read this book just as "Kellan's Story," nothing amazing will happen in your life.

The point of my sharing is to give all this to you, and then ask, plead, and even demand you ask yourself the questions they generate.

Examples could be:

Who do YOU need to be to create the life you want?

Who do YOU need to be to see yourself in your true power and possibility?

Who do YOU need to be to forgive everyone everything?

Who do YOU need to be to forgive yourself so you can access your power?

Who do YOU need to be to change whatever you want to change?

Who do YOU need to be to embrace yourself with wild self-love?

Who do YOU need to be to create a life of service and joy by serving with YOUR gifts?

Who do YOU need to be to serve everyone in your life with pure love?

Third, I am a coach. I have committed to help as many people as I can delve into the mysteries of their own motivations and being-ness. Understanding our ability to create every aspect of our lives is infinitely powerful. Indeed, we create our lives moment to moment, either intentionally or ignorantly.

More than anything, I love helping people succeed, and succeed beyond their wildest dreams. Our limited ability to dream and believe is the core barrier to living a life of purpose, prosperity and joy, every day we breathe.

This book is the final chapter in a four-part series. It begins on June 9, 2018, when I died. That is, my heart stopped in the ICU of the University of Alberta Hospital in Edmonton. During that time and the 17 days of coma that followed, I had three conversations with God at the door between life and eternity.

That experience is shared in *Meeting God at the Door – Conversations, Choices, and Commitments of a Near-Death Experience.* What happened then and in the next nine months spawned a host of other learnings. As you might expect, these mountain-moving truths are shared in still other books.

Following Meeting God at the Door is part II: The Book of Context – Break Free from the Past, Live Powerfully in the Present, Create an Amazing Future. Part III is Walking Without Fear – Letting Go of Self and Living in the Joy of What Is.

Each of those books come directly from the other-worldly experience and related events that happened between June 2018 and February 2019. Nothing that happened in my life before would have led me to expect those extraordinary events and discoveries.

In the nearly five years following *Walking Without Fear*, much has happened to refine and solidify everything that occurred during that extraordinary period. My entire life has been filled with diligent discovery and practice of all I learned and continue to explore.

This final volume puts together all the principles I have discovered, the applications I have refined and the certainty I have about your ability to live every single day in absolute joy.

That may sound impossible, but it isn't. Whether you believe it or not, you create your life, either accidentally or on purpose. This is an explanation of what I've learned about how to do that in a joyful and powerful way.

Most of all, it is an invitation to explore your own divine nature, gifts, and infinite creativity.

The choice and control are yours. I invite you to share your light, manifest miracles, and add good to the world.

Prologue

The mattress was soaking wet. At first, I wondered if I had somehow brought a large container of water to bed and spilled it. I remembered I didn't, and there was no container in the room.

What else could cause such a flood? Had I peed the bed? No, no smell, and way too much liquid for peeing the bed. Could it be sweat? The room wasn't hot, and I did not have a fever. Besides there was too much liquid for that to be the answer.

I could wring out the sheets. I could think of no explanation, so I let it go as one more impossible thing. I had just awakened from being somewhere out-of-body for nearly 18 hours. The power of that experience dwarfed the question about the liquid squishing under my body.

My mattress was ragged because just a few weeks earlier I sliced it open. During one of many drug binges, I hallucinated someone was in the mattress and struggling to get out. So, I sliced it open on the side, all the way around. Like slicing a biscuit open before toasting. No one was inside.

After the hallucination episode, I still needed something to sleep on so I put the mattress back together as best I could and ordered a new one, but it hadn't come in yet. My life was just as big a wreck as the sliced open mattress.

Forgetting the question I couldn't answer, I pondered what had happened.

During this out of body experience, I had been witness to all the staggering suffering in my own life. Both the abuse heaped on me as a child and the suffering I had inflicted on everyone else from my decades of depression, addiction, and self-loathing.

At the conclusion of that spiritual drama, I had been invited to change. I heard a voice say, "it is enough." There was no detailed explanation or direction about what to do next. Change was required and it was up to me to make things happen.

I made a fierce determination to change. Everything. Now. All at once. I had no idea how to get started, who to talk to or where to go, but the old life was over, and I was moving in a new direction.

Though I was absolutely determined to create change, there was no way I could have predicted or understood the life-altering drama that would unfold over the next 16 years.

I did have the vague sense I better fasten my seatbelt.

Part I

Living in the Present and Loving What Is

This is woo-woo speak for most people. For most of my life, it was woo-woo speak for me. I heard it and read it and pretended to understand what it all meant. I didn't.

Not because the words are strange, but because, like anything valuable and powerful, the meaning and impact come slowly and with hard work. Pondering, meditation, application, and patience are required to fully grasp and live this truth.

The universe has been around a long time. Current estimates are somewhere around 15.7 billion years, give or take a few hundred million years. At the same time, the universe is expanding, and the rate of expansion is increasing.

This is not a book on cosmology, although that's a fun and interesting topic. I mentioned the current thinking about the age of the cosmos to illustrate the fact that we are only aware of some impossibly tiny fraction of the whole of existence.

We see a microscopic fraction of what is, yet that fraction fills our entire awareness and spans our horizon. We live under the illusion that somehow we should be able to control all those externalities, so what is present in our bubble of awareness is exactly as we wish.

This is obviously impossible and unreasonable, yet we behave as if somehow our desires should control all that infinite movement and produce a path through space and time that is to our liking.

Funny, when you think about it.

If we come down out of the cosmos and just focus on the world, we notice the same thing. There are countless events and circumstances all over the world which are completely outside our awareness. Those events unfold without any intervention or influence from our consciousness.

Even in our own house or office, things are taking place in other rooms or on other floors of the building completely outside our consciousness. Therefore, they have no bearing on our present circumstance.

The truth is we have little impact on the universe as it unfolds, the thoughts and behaviours of others in the world, or the thoughts, intents, and actions of people directly in our tiny sliver of reality.

This section presents what I learned about living in and creating from the present moment. The present moment is the only one I have. All energy thinking about the past or being uncomfortable about the vagaries of the future is completely wasted and clouds your divine power of choice.

This section also reflects my journey in learning to love what is, exactly as it is. That allows me to recapture all the hoping, raging and other useless energy spent questioning or demanding certain circumstances in the flow of reality.

If we choose to love everything around us, exactly as it is, while at the same time understanding and cherishing our ability to affect whatever is in this moment, and nothing else, all our energy can be directed intentionally and be powerfully productive in adding good to the world and creating purpose, prosperity, and joy for our own lives and those around us.

This might sound a bit crazy, or at the very least unattainable, but it isn't. It is an infinitely powerful stance from which to explore your own life and your ability to use your divine gifts to lift and bless the lives of others.

This is your invitation to explore these truths to see what they mean and how they can help you be who you want to be.

Chapter 1

What Is "Living in the Present" Anyway?

After dying in June 2018 and nearly dying again in December 2018, I have a completely different perspective about what it means to be alive. The details of those experiences are in *Meeting God at the Door* and *Walking Without Fear*, so I won't repeat the stories.

Like many, I lived my life striving for what I thought I was "supposed to do." For me, that lasted 52 years. I spent all my time thinking and worrying about things that had happened yesterday, last week, or last year and fearing what uncertainties and problems tomorrow might bring. I was consumed by what I thought others thought of me.

I can't count the number of mistakes that I made, people I hurt lies I told, and other embarrassing things that filled my closet like untold skeletons. I lived in mortal fear that "tomorrow" someone would find out some of these things, and my whole life would come tumbling down.

Though I was financially successful and had powerful positions in my chosen industry, everything felt uncertain, and I never knew how long anything would last.

To camouflage the fear and uncertainty, I lived boisterously in the present, buying things for show and participating in life excessively. Somehow, I believed that all this excess and noise would quiet the raucous crowd inside my head and my heart.

It didn't.

No matter what is going on around you, you have a choice about what you focus on. You can direct your awareness and thinking. Despite external pressure to believe otherwise, you only have three things. Your time, attention, and love constitute the sum of your creative power.

Living in the present is a choice to use that time, attention, and love to focus on what is present before you in this moment and what you can do in the now.

While past events shape what is before you now, they can't be changed. You only need an accurate acknowledgment of what those events have created in this moment.

What others are doing, saying, or thinking also affects what is in front of you now. However, you don't control those things. Each of those realities affects what is before you at this moment. However, we give far too much weight and attention to things we do not know for certain and cannot control. That wasted attention takes away from our power in the present.

What happens in the future is out of your control, though you do exert influence. It is wonderful to have goals, aspirations, and to focus on the direction you want to go. We dilute our ability to achieve these goals and aspirations when we worry about what others will think and do. Consequently, we waste enormous time and energy trying to control the future.

Focusing your time, attention, and love fully and completely on who you can be and what you can do in this moment, considering all that is present in the now, is the most powerful thing you will ever do.

Time is our first tool. In our present reality, time passes unalterable forward in a linear fashion. Each moment happens once, and when it is gone, however you spent it, is complete. You can do something else with the next moment, but the one that is passed is gone forever.

Attention is our second tool. Attention is our ability to direct the power of our intellect, emotion, and intention. Like light and other electromagnetic radiation, it is most useful when focused. Far too often, we split our attention into little pieces by pretending to multitask, half-listening, and engaging in other distractions that simply dilute our power.

Love is the third tool. I use that word to represent intensity. How big are your desires, yearnings, wishes and every other aspirational word? Love is the intensity with which we use our time and attention. Half-hearted focus on anything is useless and rarely produces value.

Living in the present is a learned skill. It is a choice in each moment to be where you are and when you are. It is a powerful stance to be aware of intentionally and choose what you do with your time, attention, and love.

Chapter 2

What Do I Control?

The short answer is "not much."

The better answer is "everything that matters."

The skill of living in the present has several parts. The first is to fully understand the scope of our individual control.

We control far less than we believe and incalculably less than we wish.

It is a blessing of divine design that our span of control is so tiny. If we even remotely controlled all we wished, the chaos would be orders of magnitude beyond what we experience today, as overlapping agendas fought to order reality to their own liking.

Stop for a moment and consider what you actually control.

You control what you say. Perhaps you have habits of muttering under your breath without thinking. It is still under your control. You may habitually shout at others when they cut you off on the freeway. It is still under your control. Maybe you have a running monologue in your head about all sorts of things. It is still under your control. Let me repeat… It is still under your control.

Each of those are learned habits that you can change. It may seem hard to control what you say, but in the end, nobody can move your mouth or control your internal dialogue except you.

You control what you think. I don't mean you control every random thought that pops into your head. Stored memories and random sensory inputs create thoughts that float around.

You do control what you think about. You control where you focus your attention and what you allow to stay on the stage of your mind. Uninvited thoughts can be escorted out instantly or allowed to float away undisturbed. Again, that may be a skill you need to develop, but it is within your sovereign and individual control.

You control what you do. You may have impulses to run to strike or do other things that seem automatic and uncontrollable. They are within your control. You may have habits to change, but it is all in your control. That precious power is yours.

The most important thing you control is your attitude about any of this. Consider each of the three things you control through the lens of attitude.

If you furiously fight to bite your tongue and not say some cutting retort, that unspoken comment represents your current thinking. You can fight with it or examine the corrosive thinking and avoid the perpetual white-knuckle fight to keep your mouth in line.

If you choose to become a person who speaks only truth and kindness, and you cultivate a habit of refraining from bitter or angry vitriol, you eliminate the white-knuckle fight. Kindness becomes a natural consequence of who you are.

Controlling your thinking is perhaps the most difficult of the three things you control. It is also the most powerful and most rewarding. If you avoid the work required and fill your mind with stories of "that's just who I am," or "they deserve whatever they get," or some variation of that reasoning, then you're finished before you start.

On the other hand, if you regularly practice choosing what thoughts to keep and which ones to escort off the stage, soon it becomes a habit, and your attitude is formed naturally by what you allow on the stage of your mind and heart.

Your right to choose your stance toward life, every person, every event and nature, the cosmos, and God is perhaps your most precious sovereign possession. Yet, like I used to, many abdicate that right to choose and allow others, circumstances, and old stories to run the show.

Controlling what you do is exactly the same. If you do something angrily or with resentment, it produces the chemistry of anger and resentment. That chemistry is corrosive and medically proven to shorten your life, curb your creativity and make you a miserable cuss to be around.

On the other hand, if you practice and choose an attitude of joy regardless of your chosen action, you cultivate the chemistry of joy which is creative, rewarding and filled with light.

I prepare my taxes with what attitude? I handle a difficult conversation with what attitude? I make choices about what I do when no one is watching with what attitude?

Controlling your attitude, stance, or "who you are being" is the most vital choice you make and the most powerful skill in the universe to develop. If you abdicate that choice, the defaults created by the world around you and others limit your growth, joy, and ability to create.

Chapter 3

What Don't I Control?

If the list of things I do control is short, then the list of things I don't control is ridiculously long. I'll just give examples of categories of things we don't control so you get the picture of the enormity of this collection.

I don't control the weather. I start with that because it's so obvious. Yet, we hear and perhaps often utter complaints aimed at God or anyone within earshot that the weather is not as we wish and is interfering with something we want to do.

I don't control hurricanes, floods, heat waves, droughts, and other extreme weather elements. We are discovering that our behavior as a society influences these things, but the creator sets the laws governing their behavior. Though we may rail or mourn at the consequences, we do not control these things.

I don't control the economy. What I say or do may have some minuscule impact on my local circumstances, but beyond that, the economy is moved by macro forces far outside my ability.

I don't control the government. I can vote, lobby, and volunteer for candidates or causes, but at the end of the day, the government, laws, and enforcement mechanisms are beyond my purview. People who try to circumvent or violate this truth by taking matters into their own hands are subject to the same laws they violate.

I don't control gravity. Gratefully, it operates exactly the same every day. If it didn't, everything in the world would fall apart instantly. At the same time, we complain about our weight, which is funny because we control our eating and exercise, which creates gravity and affects our mass.

I don't control the other laws of physics, such as zero-point energy, quantum fluctuations, the speed of light, the behavior of the electromagnetic spectrum, and processes that control the creation of useful things like iPhones, computers, and satellites.

We study these laws and increase our knowledge and ability to use them for our benefit (and sometimes our destruction). Still, we have absolutely zero control over the laws that govern these wonders. The creator of all things sets those.

I don't control earthquakes, sunspots, volcanic eruptions, the Earth's magnetic fields, or anything else like those forces. Again, we study this for understanding and protection, but we control nothing.

This list is not exhaustive but representative of both the number and magnitude of things I don't control. That lack of control does not reduce our ability or willingness to complain, vilify, and blame these forces for everything that's wrong in our lives.

Perhaps you can fill in this list with many other things you don't control yet complain about. Pointing the finger at externalities allows us momentary comfort and a false sense of relief from the truth that we create our own lives.

What is important is not the thing itself or the law itself, whether natural or manufactured – what matters is my relationship to the thing. As described in the previous chapter, that relationship is 100% in my control and the source of infinite creative power.

Listing the things I don't control is not intended to be discouraging. If I adopt the point of view "I control nothing, so what's the use," I abdicate the truth of my own power.

Our individual experience every moment of every day is created by what we think and believe. What we choose to think and believe about each of these forces, laws, and circumstances is the substance from which our life experience is created.

Choosing to accept this truth is in your control. Starting with that taps into your sovereign ability to create your life experience and have perpetual joy.

Chapter 4

What Others Do

In the previous chapter, I intentionally omitted one gigantic thing we do not control. I left it out on purpose because it deserves a separate discussion. Perhaps one of the most challenging things to learn is I don't control what anyone else thinks, feels, or does.

It's far easier to agree we don't have control over the laws of physics or nature. Those laws are impersonal, and we just don't control them. On the other hand, we might believe because others are human like us, they should think like us, feel like us, and do what we believe they should do.

Or maybe it has nothing to do with the fact that they are human and should be like us. Perhaps it is just about what we want to experience as we move through the world. We want others' thoughts, feelings, and actions to provide us with that experience.

We mistakenly believe what someone else thinks, feels, and controls our experience. That is a fundamental misunderstanding of how we create our life experiences and reality.

We do not control any part of anyone's thoughts, feelings, or actions, though we are taught otherwise. Our language betrays us when we say, "He or she made me so angry," or any other sentence that puts the cause of our feelings outside ourselves.

Each person's beliefs, definitions, experiences, expectations, and perceptions define what they think, feel, and do. In an attempt to control these things, countless hours and untold money are wasted trying to control what people think and feel.

Advertising, marketing, negotiation, persuasion tactics, intimidation, and even force are methods employed to manipulate other people's thinking, feelings, and behavior. All these methods may appear effective in the short term, but at the end of the day, each of us has an absolute sovereign right to choose what we think, feel, and do.

You can persuade, request, demand, and even try to force someone into thinking, feeling, and doing what you want. Even when there is some success, the final decision is the sovereign purview of each individual.

Ultimately, we are left in precisely the same position respecting others' thoughts, feelings, and behavior as we are with the externalities described in the previous chapter.

People think what they think, feel what they feel, and do what they do. You can react without thought and abdicate your right to choose your response, or you can intentionally choose. Since you don't control what someone thinks, feels, or does, your only effective strategy is to define and choose your relationship with the thoughts, feelings, and behaviors of others.

Living in the present and loving what is will be best accomplished by focusing on things you do control and then intentionally and effectively creating the relationship you wish with the things you don't control.

Any energy, vitriol, pandering, patronizing, bribing, violence, or other action directed toward the laws of physics, the laws of nature, or the behavior of others will not create meaningful change or control of those things. Regardless of temporary appearances, it is wasted energy.

This is not a reason to give us and sulk. We can participate, persuade, and invite changes we desire. Politics and government can be changed. Laws of physics and nature can be understood and effectively channeled. Individuals and groups can be listened to, understood, persuaded, reasoned with, and perhaps effectively influenced.

The most powerful stance from which to accomplish any of these is love, creativity, and compassion. The emotions and feelings at the highest end of the spectrum bring more results, producing them faster and more lasting than any other approach to creating change.

Chapter 5

WITOT

There is another peculiar category of things that is almost mythical in power. It wields a frightening ability to manipulate your thoughts, feelings, and actions. It twists and distorts your perceptions and your willingness to try things. It rarely operates for a positive effect. For all its terrifying power, it is nevertheless imaginary and intangible.

If this sounds like the stuff of wizardry and legend, it is. At the same time, the effects are real, and they cannot be ignored. It does not exist in the real world; it only inhabits the regions of the mind.

The coronavirus exploded on the world stage in December 2019. By March 2020, it was declared a worldwide emergency and then a pandemic. Statistics were everywhere about the effects, the number of cases, deaths, and the mortality rate.

Though I had been talking about the power and effects of this last monster that keeps us from creating the ultimate life for many years, the COVID-19 pandemic gave me an idea for both the name and a comparison.

I named this terrifying disease the WITOT fungus. I often say to people that the WITOT fungus kills more people than COVID ever will. I use that comparison because it illustrates the powerful and devastating nature of the problem.

WITOT is an acronym, and it stands for "What I Think Others Think." Now that I have unveiled the truth, you may think the comparison is overblown and perhaps ridiculous.

It isn't.

Though physical death is not generally caused by WITOT, being infected with this "fungus" has caused more regret, lost opportunity, faded dreams, and ultimately more wasted potential than anything I have seen or can imagine.

We don't know what others think. Even when they speak, we are never sure they have said exactly what they think, or that we've understood what they meant. Here is the root of the problem. We don't know what others think. We can't control what they think; ultimately, what they think doesn't matter.

We spend staggering amounts of time and worry in the make-believe world of others' thinking. We are concerned about their judgment, their gossip, their comparisons, and a host of other subtle nuances. This worry dramatically reduces our ability and willingness to create.

Several problems arise when we allow the WITOT fungus to control our thinking and behavior. First, we seem naturally inclined to assume the worst. We imagine that whatever anyone thinks, it must be horrible, judgemental, and somehow correct.

We attribute unerring accuracy to the judgments and thinking we imagine is floating around in the minds of others. If we somehow believe their thinking is incorrect, we still believe it carries undue weight in the universe and controls things.

Second, we imagine others have time and energy to think about us, our efforts, and our intentions and are mainly focused on our embarrassment and failure. Everyone is looking at us, noticing whatever flaw we think we have, and all these people around us are prowling and waiting for the opportunity to pounce and destroy.

This is seldom true. Even if it is, it has nothing to do with us.

Third, we waste enormous time thinking, saying, and acting in ways we believe will mitigate or eliminate this terrible onslaught of imagined energy. We dress a certain way, say or don't say certain things, and attempt or avoid different activities.

In my experience, I have known people who skipped vacations, didn't go on group activities, stayed at home in fear, refused to make posts on social media, belittled or diminished their own value and possible contribution, and in short, lost staggering opportunities for both service and cash, all drained by the energy produced from this disease.

I'm certain you already know a dozen examples from your own life and the lives of people you know where the WITOT fungus has caused considerable damage.

Let's shed some light on this situation.

First, you have no idea what others are thinking. Regardless of their language or actions, there is always room for considerable variation and misunderstanding of that thinking because it's easy to misinterpret someone's words, body language, actions, and any other expression of said thinking.

Second, whatever someone is thinking has nothing to do with you. That may sound confusing and untrue. Consider that whatever someone is thinking comes through the lens of their own BDEEP (Beliefs, Definitions, Experiences, Expectations, and Perceptions.)

That is true 100% of the time. It must be true because the only lens each of us has is the lens of our own experience. It is impossible to see any piece of the world through any other lens than our own unless you have learned to make a concerted effort to recognize the effects of that lens.

Whatever someone is thinking is a product of their experience. Whatever you said, did, failed, or succeeded at is interpreted by their lens. That means their thinking is likely wildly different than your intention or someone else's understanding of exactly the same situation.

Third, for the most part, people don't sit around thinking about you. Everyone is busy with their situation, challenges, aspirations, and, sadly, their version of the WITOT fungus. Consider your own life. How much time do you spend thinking about someone else?

Fourth, what other people think of you is none of your business. I think that statement is attributed to Byron Katie, although I have heard it in many different places. This is an extension of the second point above.

You don't know their BDEEP, you aren't connected to their motivations and desires. You can't control any of those things. Spending any time at all worrying erodes your creativity, your willingness to live full out, and the joy you can experience in life.

Obviously, effective and accurate communication is critical for excellence when you are working with someone, working for someone, or are a leader of people. This means you must strive for accurate and well-understood communication. There are many strategies for open, honest, and effective communication. This book isn't written to teach those strategies, so if your need is for powerful and effective communications, that is an area for your exploration and growth.

Even with the most excellent communication skills, if the poison tentacles of assumptions that flow from the WITOT fungus affect your communication, then that is a powerful and fruitful area of growth you can explore.

The WITOT fungus is a major detractor from our ability to live in the present and love what is. Any time you spend twisting in the wind of the terror of your imagination, you are missing the opportunities available in the present.

Worrying about what someone is or isn't thinking is a surefire recipe for fear of what is instead of loving what is. This is because you have imagined a present with no basis in truth.

I invite you to examine your life, moment to moment. How much time are you spending somewhere besides the present moment? How much energy are you using to focus on the things you do control? How much energy are you wasting focusing on things you don't control? How significant is the energy drain from the infection of the WITOT fungus in your life?

Don't just ask these questions, take time to think deeply and make an honest assessment of your own situation. This is key to moving forward, making changes, and creating a life of Purpose and Power.

Chapter 6

What Is a Moment?

We use the word moment all the time. The definitions vary. The dictionary defines a moment as: "a brief segment of time." Another definition goes back to the ninth century, when a monk, St. Bede, seems to have defined a moment as 90 seconds.

For the purposes of our conversation, I'm going to give you a definition of a moment that I use. In creating this definition, I considered the following things that are true for me:

1. A moment isn't very long.
2. A moment has to be long enough to mean something.
3. A moment can't be a fraction of a second or a time so small it has little meaning.
4. A moment has to be long enough to focus attention.

With those things in mind, I defined a moment I enjoy that serves me very well in my pursuit to live in the present moment and love what is.

My calculations are these: there are 60 seconds in a minute, 60 minutes in an hour, and 24 hours in a day. If you multiply these together, you get 86,400. (60x60x24 = 86,400.)

As I considered this whole thing, I decided there should be 10,000 moments in a day. After all, moments are short enough that every day should have lots of them. Yet they must be long enough that "living in the present moment" means something. I also thought if the moment were too long, then the term "the present" is compromised.

Anyway, for my calculations, I divided 86,400 by 10,000 and came to 8.64 seconds. My definition of a moment is 8.64 seconds. You can say 8 ½ seconds or 9 seconds, but the idea is this period of time is a moment.

I love that definition for several reasons. First, it is short enough to really feel like "just a moment." Our attention and focus can shift so rapidly that living "present in the moment" requires significant choice and effort.

Try it right now. Look at a clock and watch nine seconds go by. Do it again. Now that you have a sense of the interval, without watching the clock, simply be in this moment for about that period of time.

Notice what your mind does. Notice if it flies all over the place or stays present. Meditation tools, like focusing on the breath, a single picture, a candle, a joyful memory, or other powerful image, can assist you in learning this discipline of controlling the mind.

Like a wild horse, every movement has staggering power and amazing beauty. When a horse is trained and connected with a loving rider, a beautiful bond forms, and there is complete focus in that connection. Those of you who have not had experience with horses may not understand, so substitute some other bond, perhaps with a dog or other beloved creature.

Because the attention and affection of animals is 100% pure, this is easy to imagine. You can create total focus, if only for a moment. Practice this in the simplest way you can imagine to begin to master the tendency of your mind to dance here and there.

Second, it is long enough to really get your teeth into. As you did the exercise, you might notice it feels like a long time, even though it is only nine seconds. Time exists for us only in this reality. We have no idea how time is measured or occurs to participants in another reality.

To avoid wandering into these esoteric realms, let's talk about how long nine seconds really is. It is about the length a world-class runner requires for a hundred metres. It is breathtakingly long when we sit with anticipation and focus on a singular event whose outcome we don't control.

Nine seconds is long enough for some event, such as an accident or an explosion, to completely change the world for untold numbers of people. If physical consequences can be of such magnitude in nine seconds, the infinitely greater power of your mind can do exponentially more.

Third, by creating a definition, it creates a practice where you can choose to master your thinking and thus begin to understand and use the limitless power of your mind and spirit.

Explore this and see what it can do for you. Create your own definition if you like. Regardless of your definition, learning to focus and explore the power of a moment is amazing.

Chapter 7

Can I Really Just Focus on a Moment?

The short answer is yes.

The long answer is still yes and involves choice and practice. I often talk with clients about focus, meditation, and our ability to remain present to and focused on what's right in front of us.

I regularly hear comments like, "My mind is just too busy; I can't do that." Sometimes it sounds like, "I tried this before, but it doesn't work, and I don't see any practical reason to spend a lot of effort trying to learn something that feels so silly."

I have no doubt those thoughts are absolutely true for that person at that moment. What they mean is they have not yet developed the ability to direct their thinking or experienced the powerful benefits of that skill.

Like any skill, you can't benefit from the developed skill until after you develop it. It takes time and effort. For encouragement, you must rely on me or others who have developed this skill and attest to its benefits.

To help you answer the question, "Can I really just focus on a moment?" It might help to start with a different question. "What do I need to do, or who do I need to be, so I can focus on a moment and reap the benefits of that practice?"

Your answer will be what you choose. Some phrases to get you started might be:

- I choose to be that I love myself.

- I choose to be that I believe in my ability to develop a new skill.
- I choose to be that I remember another helpful skill I developed.
- I choose to be that I practice regularly.
- I choose to be that I create time to make this happen.
- I choose to be that I have fun with this.

There are many more possibilities.

Each of these sentences starts with "I choose to be that…" That is important because everything starts and ends with who we are being in any given moment. Another way to describe this idea is our attitude or belief about any practice or behavior.

It has been said, "If you think you can or you think you can't, you're right." Besides being a well-worn phrase, it is an eternal truth. Doctors everywhere say the single biggest determinant in a patient's recovery is their attitude or belief about recovery.

If you believe you can't do this, it will be difficult, if not impossible, to change what you are doing now and learn a new skill. If you start with "maybe I can do this," repeated experimentation will reveal this is all well within your possibility.

Often, we get stuck in a story that sounds like: "That's just the way I am." A more accurate truth is, "These are the habits I have had for however long, and consequently, this is my current behavior. I choose to believe this cannot change and therefore, I define this attitude or behavior as a permanent part of my character and being rather than a temporary condition." There are worlds of difference between these two expressions.

The first describes our current habits, personality traits, behaviors, and attitudes as though they were permanent fixtures that cannot be changed. The second acknowledges while we are currently in the habit of behaving or thinking certain things, everything is subject to change.

Constant change is the way of the universe. Nothing stays the same except God and Eternal Truth. If you stick with the original beliefs, what changes over time is how deeply they are entrenched and the level of havoc they create.

You can learn to focus on the moment before you if you choose to develop that skill. Start small by creating some experiments to change your current thinking and behavior. Get help from a good coach for encouragement and clarity and to maintain consistency in your practice.

Chapter 8

Why Would I do THAT?

Another powerful motivator and enabler to learn to "live in the present and love what is," is to answer the following questions powerfully.

- Why would I do THAT?
- Why would I go through the effort of learning this skill?
- What will it do for me?

I won't tell you that you must do this. I won't tell you that you should do this. I will tell you the benefits I experience and that clients notice when this skill is part of life. I can also promise many of these benefits will accrue to you as well.

First benefit. Stress evaporates. You will be surprised how much time you spend thinking about what has gone before or what is yet to come. You can't do anything about either of those.

If there is a problem in the present from something in the past, you can choose to repair it. That is completely different than feeling guilty, embarrassed, or paralyzed about the past event. Clouding the present with those feelings as you choose how to do the repair limits your judgment and ability.

If something wonderful is in the past, you can choose in the present to enjoy it. That is different than yearning for the past to remain and never change. Clouding your joy with the longing for what is finished makes it less powerful because it's mixed with grief.

When you focus on the current moment (8.64 seconds), it's very clear what you can and can't do. Choosing to focus on and do the things you can is more effective, and it eliminates all stress that comes from spending your precious time, attention, and love on things you cannot control.

Even in seemingly difficult or negative situations, where things are painful or delicate, staying clearly focused on what you can do in this moment, reduces suffering, increases focus, and lowers stress.

Second benefit. Creativity explodes. Creativity is stifled when we focus on things we can't control because as soon as we think of something, we are overwhelmed with all the reasons we can't do it right this minute.

Perhaps you're not in the right place, or you're not with the right people, or you don't have access to something necessary at that moment. That creates negative pressure on your ideation and your willingness to create what you want to be.

When you focus only on the moment, you realize you have far more options than you first imagine. Ideas will flow that otherwise would have remained hidden behind the energy of "can't, "won't," and "doesn't."

My own experience and that of clients is by continually returning to the moment and what we can do in the here and now, ideas flow, and new possibilities emerge. In this very moment, you have creativity beyond your wildest understanding. Mainly, you don't see it unless you have learned to look deeply and fiercely into the here and now.

Third benefit. Patience increases. This might feel counterintuitive because it may seem limiting when you focus only on what you control right here and now. The opposite is true.

When you focus solely on what is available in the here and now, clarity emerges about the sequencing of growth. Whether you are fixing a problem or creating something amazing, everything grows at its own pace.

Trees don't grow overnight. Your impact in the world using your gifts and hard-won experience grows gradually. They don't suddenly exist. Your growth trajectory will elevate as you narrow your focus to the here and now.

Training yourself to do what is here and leave alone what isn't here brings a sense of peace and order, even if you are creating a universe. In one place in sacred Scriptures, there is an interesting sentence describing God's behavior during this time.

He issued a command to create something about the cosmos, and the scripture notes, "He watched until he was obeyed." Even in that circumstance of Almighty power, patience existed and was a fundamental part of the eternal creation.

Fourth benefit. Power expands. When you do what's in front of you, you have far more likelihood of success. You are using your own power that exists in the here and now. You are using the resources on hand in the present moment. When you do this, your success increases dramatically.

How many times have you tried to do something you thought was important, and you failed because the right people, resources, attitude, circumstances, or other requirements were not here in the present moment or couldn't be accessed?

This success is self-reinforcing. The more success you experience, the more confident you are in future endeavors. Your power, your confidence, your certainty in the outcome, and your knowledge about how to handle things all increase. I have witnessed this unfold in all kinds of extraordinary ways.

Yet, with all this awesome opportunity, most have not yet disciplined themselves to live in the present, act in the present and love everything about this moment, right here, right now.

Chapter 9

Resistance to What Is

The last several chapters dealt with living in the present moment. The next three chapters will deal with "loving what is." Like living in the moment, loving what is could be considered a cliché and a painful statement of a hopeless reality instead of an empowering choice.

In the introduction to part one, I talked about how long the universe has been around and how little of it we know. Indeed, an incomprehensibly small fraction.

At the same time, we seem obsessed with the need to control everything that is part of what we do notice, even though that is both impossible and ultimately undesirable. Unimaginable chaos would result if we each controlled all our circumstances to our whims.

I must reiterate the distinction between controlling circumstances to our liking and the moment-to-moment creation of the experience of our lives. We absolutely control our life experiences by our attitudes and choices. We control very little of our external circumstances.

Though we don't control our circumstances, we choose how we view, experience, and handle that reality. One way to meet reality is to resist furiously. Resistance can take several forms. We can actively fight against reality, deny the reality before us, or sullenly sulk as we swim in the sea of injustice and bad luck.

The following picture illustrates the range of attitudes or states of being towards what is. Let's call it the Reality Response Line, or RRL. Obviously, there is a range of attitudes and words we can use to describe the resistance at the left end of the RRL. There is also overlap between the resistance end of the line and the acceptance position in the middle.

ResistingAcceptingEmbracing

The hallmarks of choosing to be at the left end of the RRL are clear and mostly unpleasant. They range from acts of violence, sabotage, and active defamation to bitter complaining to anyone, everyone, and no one in particular. You may know someone who lives like this all the time, or you may personally have taken this approach to life.

Examples of this approach include:

- Complaining about the weather and how sudden storms have trashed a vacation.
- Rage about how greedy and uncaring capitalists have caused climate change and made the summer so much hotter.
- Angry lashing out at the government or opposing political parties.
- Railing against those who have a different worldview and blaming them for the failings in society, safety, and personal freedoms that fall outside your view of how things ought to be.
- Ripping a business partner because they have done something you view as betrayal, and suddenly, you find yourself completely obliterated financially.
- Intentional destruction of a life partner who is unfaithful or leaves a relationship and leaves you emotionally devastated.
- Becoming utterly destroyed by the illness or death of someone who may have been close to you.
- Inconsolable grief at how unfair everything is.

- Railing at God because He should not allow "this" to happen.
- Amassing massive debt because you want what you want right now, and the stupid, rotten, unfair system doesn't allow you to make enough money to get ahead and enjoy your life like you think you should be allowed to do.

This is a small sampling of the different ways this anger and denial manifest. To be clear, feeling dissatisfaction with a current situation and then moving the levers you control to make change is reasonable and expected. That is not what I'm talking about.

Take some time right now to think of your favorite example. Someplace in your life where some outside force has negatively affected you, and your immediate and strong reaction is to blame, pass judgment, and perhaps even try to exact revenge.

You rage, blame, and finally collapse in exhaustion and simply capitulate because you have no control and can't change anything. Finally, you sullenly just try to stick out each day and hope tomorrow, next month, next year, next job, or next spouse will give you a better break.

This is the stance of resistance, denial, or fighting with what is. This includes an attitude of "surrender with bitterness." It is blaming everything outside of you for your circumstance and frequently using the words "if they would just…" And everything else is all outside yourself.

You know life has given you a raw deal and you stare jealously or angrily at those who seem to have things better than you do. You feel you are often the victim of negative behaviors and happenstance and don't understand why you got dealt such a bad hand.

I have intentionally described this with fairly extreme examples. Maybe your life right now is in the midst of one of these very difficulties. Whether you are having a really hard time right now or are experiencing life in its normal shape, there is an opportunity to live in the spirit of denial and resistance.

You choose to feel powerless, blame others, and spend nearly all of your time hating the present, thinking back to good old days or hoping for better future days. This approach doesn't work well and life goes around in the same old circle.

Put the book down and take another moment to consider areas in your life where this resistance is true in a more subtle way than the hard-core examples we started with. Let's say you're driving to work. (We do that a lot less these days with so much more remote work after the Covid-19 pandemic, but this example will work nicely anyway.)

On your way to work, traffic is heavy, there is unexpected construction, and there is a rude jerk who cuts you off and makes you miss your exit because they seem to be in a hurry and think they own the road.

First, you might rage, then try to think of an alternative route, and then you slump back in the seat, simply resigned to your bad luck. Traffic problems are a worn-out stereotype, but they still represent the feeling of helplessness and resistance to external events.

If you live in a stance of denial and resistance to what is, your heart is primarily heavy; you're mostly angry, frustrated, or resigned, creativity is low, and your chances of creating a powerful life and loving what is approach zero.

Unfortunately, this is the stance of many people. It doesn't have to be. This moment, you have a choice and the power to view the same external circumstances in different, more empowering, and more creative ways.

Chapter 10

Accepting What Is

Another possibility about how to energetically face the externalities you don't control is "Accepting what is." In our diagram, it is the middle area of the RRL.

ResistingAcceptingEmbracing

Sometimes, I call this "the state of allowing." This is far less destructive than denial and resistance and much easier on your heart and soul, not to mention everyone around you. There are a wide range of attitudes and behaviors in this middle section, and they overlap the lower and higher choices of being.

I label the lower end of the RRL "resisting," and the higher end "embracing" because of how they affect us and those around us. At the left end, we feel more anger, bitterness, fear, and related emotions. Those emotions reduce creativity and intelligence. They limit our reasoning and our capacity for cooperation.

They also can affect those around us in a similar fashion. Emotions are contagious, and the negativity associated with resistance reduces the power of relationships and lowers the availability of our closest allies.

At the right end of the RRL, we are more prone to love, creativity, compassion, and related feelings. These increase creativity, problem-solving, cooperation, and other positive states of being.

The middle section is a large range with a variety of manifestations. You could describe your response at the left end of the middle section as "suffering in silence." Perhaps you expected the challenges you are facing or even think you deserve them.

Maybe you have come to believe you just have a tough row to hoe, and your life is to be one of suffering. Whatever your explanation, you put up with it. Each day fades into the next and you wistfully look forward to the occasional bright spots that happen from time to time.

At the higher end of this middle section, you might hear the language, "everything happens for a reason." That is a cliché phrase tossed about when bad things happen, we don't understand why, and we're trying to find consolation and move forward. A victim mindset still generates this thinking.

The common characteristic of this entire range is the idea that "I don't control anything that happens around me, so I might as well just accept things, try not to get angry or depressed, hope things get better, and figure out how to deal with life until they do."

You believe since you don't control things, the best you can do is allow them to be, or suffer through them, and make the best of each day as it goes by. That is a passive and weak stance. What is missing is a recognition and use of the control you do have over your stance or being-ness.

Examples of this middle area stance include statements like:

- It's just God's will.
- I have no choice.
- There's nothing I can do about this anyway.
- There are bigger forces at work.
- It's too hard to change things.
- It's just how I am.
- It's a result of their upbringing.
- It's the lousy system.
- It's too late now; if I had just started sooner.

- It's just not my season.

These aren't all of the phrases you might use or hear. It's enough to understand both the typical energy in this stance and the powerlessness created by choosing to believe any of those ideas.

The idea that you're just a pawn in a large game or a cog in the machine is not true. You can choose to believe that, and many do, but that doesn't mean there are no other options.

It's important to remember that this stance of acquiescence or surrender is part of many family and cultural frameworks. You are born into a certain status, and the best you can do is not make too much noise, do a good job at whatever you end up with, and carve out an acceptable life inside these limitations.

We reinforce this learned helplessness when we don't allow natural consequences of behavior to take place, or when we shield ourselves or others from the truth of our attitudes and behaviors by pointing the finger to external causes.

There is a massive difference between kindness and ignoring or pretending away real consequences. One example is a child whose parents continually rescue them from every misbehavior, thereby creating the attitude that reality and not the real world are subject to one's whims.

Movies, television, and books that present solutions to complex problems in the length of a TV sitcom reinforce the idea that everything should be easy, and that the root of all problems is "out there." When reality unfolds differently, we blame others, flop back in the recliner, and settle for crumbs.

The truth is, everyone has massive difficulties in life. One study said in an average sample, over 50% of people are going through some major upheaval in their lives at that moment.

Even the idea "everything happens for a reason," is a two-edged sword. While it suggests there is a larger intelligence and design at work, which is true, it can engender passivity, suggesting that just waiting yields the best results and the benefits of any hardship will become clear after enough time.

Sometimes that happens. My experience is that it happens, more often, more powerfully, and sooner when we actively participate in choosing how we experience every event in our lives.

One example will illustrate this point. You have a sudden and severe reversal in your health. No one is at fault; nothing explains the circumstance, yet you are severely ill for a few weeks. What do you do?

You take every reasonable action, get the proper care, and do what you are told to do with respect to recovering your health. You feel frustrated, your plans are derailed, and you wait for improvement. The passive approach leaves you suffering in silence and wondering why this happened to you.

Assuming "this happened for a reason," you might believe that eventually, whether you recover soon or after a longer time, there will be some benefit to you, which will be apparent in the future.

Now what?

It may seem like there is nothing more to do. Most people, most of the time, take this middle approach to life. To me, it feels like an addiction to mediocrity. At best, people live at the higher end of the middle range of Allowing and Surrendering and assume that's as good as it gets.

There is so much more available.

Every circumstance, every event, and every choice has awesome sauce as a possible outcome. The secret lies in the choices you make moment-to-moment as your life unfolds, and the attitude you have as you make each spiritual, mental, and physical choice.

Chapter 11

Loving What Is

Now we get to the real power. I will state it boldly, right up front and then we will talk about what it all means.

Love What IS.

This is at the right end of the RRL line we drew before. Lean in. Hug every event.

ResistingAcceptingEmbracing

Love the reality of your existence as it unfolds before you. Choose to love all the wonderfulness that happens to intersect with the tiny fraction of the universe that is your slice of life. Don't argue with it; don't just surrender to it; actively love it.

Just because you can.

You have a choice to love what is, in every circumstance, in every hour, in every minute of your life. You can love all the disasters; you can love all the betrayals; you can love all the inconveniences, and you can love all the good stuff, too.

Am I crazy to suggest such a notion?

It is NOT crazy. It is real choice, and it is empowering. Rather than taking any stance of resentment or helplessness when something is part of your circumstance, it gives you a different place to start, take control, and do everything you can with your most creative and powerful energy.

Dr. Martin Seligman wrote a book called *Learned Optimism.* Among other things, he detailed the results of a multi-decade study that followed two groups of people. One group was generally optimistic, and the other generally pessimistic.

His intention was to see what the effects were on their lives. His studies show that people who choose an optimistic outlook on life live longer, make more money, are healthier, and enjoy life more. That book is also a manual for developing the habit of being optimistic.

What is optimism? I use a very simple definition. Optimism is a choice to approach every situation with the idea "there's gotta be a way" to solve this problem. Pessimism is a choice to look at things through the lens of "we probably can't fix this."

Optimism is a good starting point to understand the idea of loving what is, but in no way encompasses the full depth of loving what is in every circumstance and with every thought.

My experience teaches me there is a divine power. This power is personal, intentional, and available. I have seen too much evidence in my life and the lives of others to settle on any other possibility. In past decades, I had doubts and fears just like everyone else. Sometimes all that "spiritual stuff" seemed irrelevant and far away. During those decades, I ignored it all.

Today, I have a certainty that increases with each passing moment. As part of my mission and my work, I talk to many people from all over the world. When people tell the truth, nearly everyone will admit to feeling intuition, nudges, and other sources of inspiration outside of themselves.

From that point of view, let's consider a couple of things. Since there is a divine creator, whatever name you choose to attach to this force, then there is a purpose to this creation. Even though we don't understand all of the nuances and purposes, it's clear that some of the design principles are:

- Opportunity for personal growth
- Freedom of choice
- Personal responsibility
- Infinite opportunity

As a divine, purposeful creation with gifts and a mission and purpose, we stand at the brink of every day and at every moment with choices about how we interpret and act in every situation.

We already know that the vast majority of circumstances around us are outside our control. We don't control others behavior, and we don't control the macro consequences of society's behavior. We don't control governments; we don't control nature, and we don't control the laws of the universe. (While there are exceptions to these rules when miraculous things happen, this is generally the truth.)

In every circumstance, without exception, we control our own thoughts, feelings, and actions with respect to every single circumstance that presents itself. Let's consider some examples.

Something happens you consider positive and in line with moving you toward your desired outcomes, whether they be financial, physical, emotional or anything else. That feels good, you may speak words of gratitude and you look forward to more of the same. Hopefully, you do as much as you can to utilize the positive events. Examples might include:

- You close some new clients.
- You get accepted into a program you've been seeking.
- You perform well at a concert, presentation, or speaking engagement.
- You have a new insight regarding your spiritual standing.
- You see a beautiful number on the scale when you weigh in this morning.

- Someone says yes when you ask them out or propose marriage.
- You're approved for the house you want to buy.
- Thousands of other possibilities.

Something happens you consider neutral or irrelevant regarding your desired outcomes in any area of life endeavor. Perhaps you ignore it, perhaps it is an irritation because it distracts you for a moment, or perhaps it doesn't even enter your field of consciousness. Examples might include:

- Your neighbor gets in a car wreck.
- A war starts overseas.
- An election in a neighboring country surprises you.
- Your city manager gets indicted for fraud.
- A large company closes their stores in a neighboring state, citing safety concerns.
- A neighboring state passes a law you detest.
- A famous person commits suicide.
- A dictator in a foreign country is assassinated.
- There are huge wildfires in another country.
- Thousands of other possibilities.

In listing these elements as neutral, I know any of them might trigger you or be cause for concern depending on your point of view, your personal experience, or other connection you might draw. They may cause you to think about things you should do to prevent a similar occurrence that would be closer to home and affect you negatively.

You might wonder if those things, while far away, might affect you anyway. You might begin to worry about something you can't do anything about because you're scared that somehow it might change the circumstances of your life, your state, your plans, or other aspects of your existence.

Perhaps these thoughts bother you, and you have conversations about them with people at work, church, community, or even grocery stores. There doesn't seem to be anything you can do, so you relegate them to the back burner, though it remains a niggling worry.

Something happens you consider negative regarding a desired life outcome in your personal, business, or other life pursuit. Here are some real-world examples of stuff that happens. These examples come from my life or the lives of clients or people I know personally.

- You have your worst-ever month in sales.
- You find out your life partner has been cheating on you.
- You find out your business partner is embezzling money.
- You find out you have cancer.
- You struggle with a long-standing addiction you can't seem to master.
- You keep trying to do more, but procrastination beats you every time.
- You make a resolution to do more marketing, but something always gets in the way.
- Someone hits your car.
- Your car gets towed while you are at a doctor's appointment.
- One of your kids gets arrested for drugs.
- Depression is just eating your lunch.
- You lose your job.
- You want to start a business, but all the "signs" say you shouldn't.

- You want to be better, but there are too many setbacks every time you start.

This is just a small fraction of things that are real-world examples. Fill in the blank with your own worst occurrence from the last 30 days. By worst, I mean the thing that was most unexpected, most damaging, or most demoralizing to your attitude.

You have a choice about how you view each of these events. The event has already happened, and nothing you can do or think changes what has occurred.

What does it look like to love what is? Loving what is asks us to look at each event as a blessing or opportunity. "What if that ____________________ (fill in the blank with your event) is the best possible thing that could have happened today? What if it is not only a "blessing in disguise" but a near-term opportunity for real progress?

Why would you want to think about things that way? First, when your mind is positive and your heart is open, you are more creative and more open to ideas. You are able to see things you can't see otherwise and make better decisions.

Second, what has happened is finished and you must create from the present reality, whether you like it or not. Any energy spent railing against the present is wasted. Choosing to be resigned to the present reality is less harmful than railing against the present, but it is far less powerful than a choice to love what is. Why would you want to do something less than the best approach to your reality?

Third, it feels way better to create and live from a positive frame of mind than it does from a negative frame of mind. You create your frame of mind, even if you haven't regularly accessed that power. So why not choose optimism, positivity, and love?

You don't need to love the person that did you wrong. You don't need to love bad things that have happened. You do have the opportunity to make a choice to be "in love" with the present moment, regardless of how you got there.

Since the purpose of our existence is to love ourselves and grow, to love and serve others, and to develop and use the gifts we have, then learning to love the present is the most creative and powerful choice you can ever make every time, all the time.

Chapter 12

Getting to Zero

The last three chapters discussed different possibilities on the RRL line, which represents the continuum of reactions to every present moment. If you have been living up to now with unconscious default reactions determined by old habits, the first thing you need to do is get to zero.

Zero is the practice of creating space for choice. Most people, most of the time, live by reaction. That reaction is determined by past experience and interpretation of present reality. We don't take time to choose the reaction because we are convinced however we react is truth and the obvious choice given the input.

Realizing there is choice in every moment may be the most awesome discovery you ever make.

We have all heard it said: "You don't see the world the way it is, you see the world the way you are." I used to hear this phrase as an indictment, meaning I was incapable of seeing reality. Instead, it is simply a statement of fact.

You can't see the world any differently than through the lenses you have, which have been created by your lifetime of experience. The illumination comes when you realize there are other lenses. Every person has their own set of lenses, and every pair of lenses are just as valid as any other.

It took me a long time to understand that idea, and even longer to accept the truth of the part that says, "any other set of lenses are just as valid as mine." If we are going to start making choices about how we react to externalities and our existing attitudes and opinions, we need a new tool.

In chapter five, I defined your BDEEP (Beliefs, Definitions, Experiences, Expectations, and Perceptions) as your default view of the world, including what is possible for you, and everything else. There's no need to fight with the fact that you have a BDEEP or that it is your default view.

All that has to happen is to recognize everybody has one and they love theirs as much as you love yours. So, what do we do with that? Let's just set it aside for a moment.

Rather than trying to convince yourself to believe something different or argue with your natural inclinations, let's do the two-step process that is the foundation of all mastery. If you want to master anything in the entire world, there are only two steps.

1. Notice.
2. Choose.

In mastering a difficult piece on the piano, I notice how it sounds, and if some mistakes or areas present difficulty. Then I choose to work out the fingering, slow the tempo down, or apply some other technique to master that part of the song, and eventually the whole piece.

Blasting onward and refusing to notice eliminates your ability to grow. Failing to choose something different means that you will stay exactly where you are. It's exactly the same with changing your BDEEP and your place on the RRL.

The first step in changing your default place on the RRL is to notice where you are in the first place. This will take some practice, but you will find very quickly you get in the habit of noticing the feelings in your body.

Every time you have any emotion connected with something that happens, something someone says, an unexpected event, changes in the weather, changes in the government, or anything that causes you to experience a feeling, stop.

Take a moment to identify what happened, and then identify what you are feeling about that thing. There will likely be multiple layers to this effort. At a minimum, there is the event itself and how you feel about the event, and there is the causal factor of the event and how you feel about that.

Let's say the boss at work makes a decision that both surprises you and is disappointing. The first feeling is whatever you believe about that unfavorable decision. The second feeling is perhaps some frustration or anger directed toward "that idiot boss" who made the decision.

I don't find it fruitful to fight with the feelings. To start with, just notice all this stuff. After you notice, then relax for a moment so you can calm down and get clearheaded. That may be all you can do to start with, depending on how deeply entrenched your habits are, and how strong the reaction is.

If you create a habit of just slowing down, noticing what you're feeling and then relaxing for a moment to let everything calm down, you have accomplished step one.

Step two is to choose. It's not effective to just tell yourself to choose a different feeling. If your reactions are strong and your habits are well entrenched, that won't work. That is like repeatedly white-knuckling some difficult process. Willpower and force don't work for very long.

Instead, ask yourself the following question: "What reaction right now would be the most effective at expressing the concerns I have and moving toward creating the changes I think need to happen?"

If you really slow down, calm down, and ask that question, it will become clear the negative reactions at the left end of the RRL won't accomplish much and may alienate those you need to work with in making change.

Reactions in the middle of the RRL won't do much either because simply living with the situation is primarily apathetic, and you're just trying to figure out how to adapt to this terrible thing that just happened.

Embracing the new reality as the leader's will is just recognizing what is true. The boss has the authority to decide and did so. Your opinion was either not considered or was not persuasive. Understanding this and then considering what needs to happen to make change is the only effective option, and it is the most powerful one.

From a place of love, kindness, and creativity, you're far more likely to create the dialogue needed to change the outcome you don't like or come to a constructive understanding of how to go forward with the new reality.

Practice getting to zero in every situation in which you feel a reaction. This becomes earlier as you practice. You will be surprised how fast you notice what you're feeling and identify the various parts of the equation. Then you can relax and consider from love and creativity what you might do next.

Chapter 13

Building From There

The "Notice-Choose" framework is helpful to master both principles in this section. Choosing to be fully present in every moment, and choosing to love what is, are simple and powerful tools for creation. If those practices are not part of your present life, or they are dusty with lack of use, now is a perfect time to master these practices.

These skills are essential for rapid growth in almost anything you are trying to do. This is especially true when you're talking about creating internal power and the ability to build a life that is full of purpose and joy.

This book is about creating a life with a driving purpose and creating the personal power to turn your vision into reality. It can be your manual for being fully engaged in the joyful process of that creation.

Living in the present moment is not a one-and-done exercise. It is something you will be mindful of and practice for the rest of your life. The longer you do it, the easier it gets, and the more it becomes your natural state of being.

Choosing to love everything that is in the world around you is another masterful skill that is never finished. It is a mountain with no top. The ever-changing world and the ebb and flow of everything around us creates a constant opportunity for practice.

I encourage you to take these principles seriously and begin an effort today to create a life consistent with being fully present in every moment and loving what is, no matter what it turns out to be.

My journey has taught me that mastery of these principles is a required part of creating the kind of life that has massive purpose and awesome power. It is an essential ingredient that takes constant refinement and sharpening.

But it is only a foundation. It is not the endgame.

As we move to the next section, I will assume you are practicing being present in every moment and learning to love your reality as it unfolds. Keep at it. It will take patience and joyful persistence. It is worth the effort. Refer to this section as often as you need to make that true for you.

Develop your own methods and your own reminders that help you stay joyfully focused on the present moment, which is the only one you have, and lean into the reality you have with all the love you can generate in your soul and receive from the divine.

Part II

Creating Your Guiding Stars

For millennia, navigation was done by the stars. Whether in the northern or southern hemisphere, there were celestial bodies whose position relative to the earth allowed them to be fixed points in the sky.

Sailors knew about where they were and the direction they were heading by referencing the stars. I'm not a navigation expert and don't know all the stars used, but in the northern hemisphere, it is the North Star, Polaris, which always indicates where Celestial North is.

It's a little more complicated in the southern hemisphere, but the southern cross can be used to locate the south celestial pole. There are a couple of different ways to get that done, and anyone who sails will know both methods.

Starting from the place of diligent effort to live and create in the present moment and learning to love what is, we can now move to the next part of living a life of purpose, prosperity, and joy. I refer to that as "The Ultimate Life."

Guiding stars, like the navigation aids of the seas, help us choose how we create life. Rather than lights in the sky, these internal stars are ideas, principles, and commitments we choose to direct our activity and creation efforts. When you live in the present, and create from a place of loving what is, your guiding stars give constant direction, so you are clear about what to create.

When you have powerful guiding stars, making decisions, choosing how and what to create, and understanding the best course of action in any situation becomes clear and simple.

There is both good news and bad news in this arrangement. As always, it depends on your chosen viewpoint. The truth is simple. You create your guiding stars. You decide who you are. You decide how you walk through the world. Either with intention or by default, it is in your hands.

It's good news because all the levers are in yours to operate. It's bad news for some because this truth takes away all opportunity to blame and escape the responsibility of this creation. Most people don't internalize this reality and, consequently, create accidentally and without real direction.

Unconscious creation comes from everywhere. Socialization from parents, community, church, society, friends, and other places present and impose directions and values externally, and that is needed for a time as we are born helpless and dependent on others for survival.

After we grow up, we can evaluate and choose who we are or just continue in the direction we were given. At the end of the day, you are an independent, divine creator and will stand or fall by your own hand. The choice to intentionally create your guiding stars is deep work, powerful medicine, and ultimately rewarding beyond any description.

Imagine for a moment knowing exactly who you are in the world, knowing exactly how you choose to behave, and what you choose to create in every circumstance. The clarity and confidence that flows from such knowledge is impossible to understand until you start doing it.

This section is about the process I used to create my guiding stars. It is the same process I use to help people I work with create their own guiding stars. I do not pretend it is the only method. I know it works, I know it produces power and confidence.

Whether you use my method or something else, the important thing is to intentionally create these guiding stars. Ignoring or pretending away the need to do this simply prolongs uncertainty, confusion, and aimless wandering in your life.

At the end of the section, I will share the documents I have created. They are not shared in the context of direction. They are shared only as an example of something that has come out of this process. For me, they are an invincible life altering daily power, day after day.

My documents change, sometimes only slightly with minor word modifications. Sometimes they change significantly as I learn more, create more, and become more in tune with the divine and the universe of opportunity in front of all of us. The power is in the work of creation.

With that understood, let's get started.

Chapter 14

Who Are You?

The most fundamental question we must consider and then answer in creating these guiding stars is a choice about who we are. This may sound confusing, because, generally, people think who they are is already decided.

Who you are at this moment is the person you have chosen to be from all the BDEEP (Beliefs, Definitions, Experiences, Expectations, and Perceptions) you have had up to this moment. Even the way you interpret this challenge is a consequence of these past experiences.

Until you look at your BDEEP intentionally and critically, all your understanding and interpretation of your life, your possibilities, and your meaning come from external influences of the past and simply reacting to the world around you.

A simple example will illustrate. You are standing in a line at the customer service desk of a busy retailer two days after Christmas. You're holding a fairly heavy bag with an item you wish to return. There are about ten people in the line in front of you.

You hear a commotion at the customer service desk, and you see an unhappy customer shouting and berating the clerk. You don't really know what's going on, but you assume based on past experience, the kerfuffle comes from the customer not getting exactly what they wanted or getting it fast enough.

The disturbance gets loud enough that eventually, a manager intervenes, and the conversation is taken elsewhere. What are you thinking? Are you feeling empathy for the clerk? Are you thinking "it's easy enough for the big outfits to take your money, but when there's a problem, it's a big pain to get it fixed?"

Are you thinking the rude customer should be arrested and put in jail, or at least slapped with a significant fine? Are you wondering what in the world is so important it requires such anger?

I'm using this example which is outside of you, to illustrate the point of this chapter. Regardless of store rules, clerk disposition, pressing appointments on the calendar of the customer, or anything else, that customer has the option, in every moment, to choose how they think, feel, and behave.

Those choices depend 100% on who they choose to be. They are unrelated to the friendliness of the clerk. They are unrelated to the rules of the store. They are unrelated to the economy, the government, the weather, God and the universe, or anything else.

If that customer chooses, because he can, "I am that I create harmony and success, regardless of what is going on around me," his or her behavior will be wildly different than if they choose "I am that I get what I deserve, and insist I'm treated a certain way, no matter what else is going on."

Most people never think of themselves or their interactions in that way. They simply enter into situations and react to whatever's going on around them. This is an unguided life. Likely, that customer is not being guided by any principles they have intentionally created and declared for themselves, but is fully reactive to the behavior of others and circumstances around them.

Answering the question "Who are you?" involves making choices about who you are being in every situation. It's impossible to know every situation that will come before you in any hour, day, and certainly a lifetime. It is possible to make declarations and choices about who you choose to be, regardless of the world around you.

At this point, you might say "But what if I get treated unfairly?" Or you might be thinking "What if I'm getting ripped off?" All those things may occur in your life. In fact, I guarantee there will be many occurrences, events, and behaviors that could offend your sense of justice and what is right.

Remember, your BDEEP is yours. It forms the context or lenses through which you see everything. Someone with a different context, in exactly the same situation, would likely have a completely different interpretation of what is "right." Their views are just as valid as yours.

Different is not worse or better. It is just different. You do not control any of that. The only thing you control in any situation is what you think, how you feel, and how you choose to act. Your thoughts, feelings, and actions are an infinite canvas of possibilities.

Controlling what you think is not about trying to eliminate random thoughts that always pop up. Those thoughts pop up unbidden from sensory input, random memories, and other sources. Instead, control means to exercise intentional oversight about the thoughts you allow to remain in your mind, or the thoughts you bring onto the stage, offer a chair, and allow to play a part in the drama of your life.

Imagine for a moment if one of your chosen declarations was "I am love." Thoughts, feelings, words, and actions would all go through the filter "what would love do?" Applying this in every moment makes choices simple and would radically alter thoughts, feelings, and actions.

It is very likely you have never created a set of firm, fire-breathing declarations you choose to govern your life. Making choices about who you are is a foundational starting point to creating your guiding stars.

Chapter 15

Where Are You Going?

A companion question to "Who are you?" is an opportunity to choose and declare where you are going. This is not a physical destination but a choice of what you will create for the outcome of your life.

We are often so focused on putting out fires right in front of us that we don't think about the long term, and we don't make conscious choices about where we are really headed.

Do you, right this minute, have a declared and specific plan for where your life is headed? This includes spiritual, physical, emotional, mental, relationship, family, and financial outcomes. Most people wander through life with vague ideas and hope they are generally leaning in the right direction.

Here is another way to think about this: with all your activity, all your thinking, all your conversations and interactions, all your work in creating wealth, all the learning and accomplishment pursuing hobbies, all the love and sacrifice caring about people, all the resourcefulness handling emergencies, and everything else, have you defined your outcomes?

Don't be discouraged if this is a strange question or if you haven't thought about it at all. Mostly, people think like this: "I'll make a lot of money, be really successful, and then I'll be happy because I can do whatever I want."

That statement simply cannot be true as it is written. It is not specific. It is inherently contradictory. It represents a terrifyingly murky landscape. It provides no blueprint from which to operate.

After you make concrete decisions and declarations about who you want to be and then answer questions like: "If I am as I declare myself to be, where will this lead?" Or "What will be the activities and outcomes I expect and intentionally create?" you have a real starting point.

Growth is the natural order of things. It is expected that we are always up to something. Intentionally picking goals is a powerful and productive habit. You don't go for a drive with absolutely no destination in mind unless the goal is to drive around, relax, and talk with no destination in mind.

Even that has purpose and intention. When you first declare who you are in the world and what characteristics and behaviors flow from that process, deciding goals is much simpler.

Twenty-five years ago, my goals centered around making as much money as I could, having the most important position I could, and having the praise of everyone around me. I accomplished those goals and was miserable. Those goals did not come from a foundation of principle. Consequently, though I achieved my financial goals, my life was a wreck.

After I declared my being, my relationship with God and the universe, my goals changed dramatically. Today, my goals are not measured in cash, although I track business performance. They are measured in the number of lives touched, the number of people helped, and how much good I can add to the world.

To be sustainable, powerful, and meaningful, your goals must be anchored to the principles that guide your life. The document, vision board, or other instruments that contains your objectives must make your heart vibrate, and your soul sing every time you look at it.

If it feels heavy, hard, or like drudgery, it will be impossible to stay focused. You will be distracted by every little thing that comes along.

You can use vision boards, written documents, video stories, or any tool that works for you to assemble the goals you have. They may change year to year as you reach some, refine some, and leave others by the wayside. The important part is to set them in the most powerful way you can, visit them every day and lean into them with love and excitement.

Chapter 16

What Is "The Underneath?"

Every person who has ever jumped into the journey of personal growth knows the feeling that comes when you think about something new and difficult. For example, you know you should lose weight, and you want to, but when you think about it, you feel sick to your stomach.

You know you should make some phone calls for your client acquisition process, but you think of all kinds of reasons not to. You go to a powerful event, get motivated by the speaker, and then you get home, and everything just slides off the plate.

"The Underneath" is a name I use to describe that sometimes subtle and sometimes overwhelming feeling of uncertainty and doubt. It is that pile of rocks that hold you back. It is that voice in your mind that tells you you're not good enough. It is the echo chamber of times you have failed to do whatever you said. It is the imposter you feel you are because people don't know the "real truth" about what's going on in your heart or your life.

It is quite common that no matter how loudly you scream, how many books you read, how many pronouncements you make, and how many new products you buy, "The Underneath" is always there with its nagging voice of doubt, fear, procrastination, and the reminder of all the things that have gone wrong in previous efforts.

I gave it this name because it always feels like it's underneath everything you try to do. Everything you think, everything you promise yourself, and every change you try to make sits on top of this squishy quicksand feeling of doubt and fear.

Sometimes, it's right up in your throat, and other times, it's just this faint knowledge something will get in your way, some doubt will surface, or some distraction will get the better of you, and it won't work. It makes you feel like all your plans are on sand and can get washed away by any wave that comes along.

Sometimes, we believe we're the only person who feels this uncertainty, which is so lonely and fearful. Perhaps we pretend it's not there. Sometimes, we feel it means there's something wrong with us, and that somehow our flaws give us this justifiably horrible self-image.

You are NOT alone. Every person who ever tried to do anything had these feelings of doubt and uncertainty. This feeling of fear is the heritage of being human and having lived, failed, and received judgment or ridicule in the school of hard knocks.

Now that you know this feeling is as common as air, let's talk about where it comes from.

Chapter 17

Where Does "The Underneath" Come From?

You are not born with fear. Babies and toddlers are essentially fearless and do things that scare their parents to death. Teenagers often feel invincible and consequently can get hurt badly or do things that were considered insanely impossible. Somewhere, we learn fear.

If we are not born with this doubt, uncertainty, and hesitancy, where does it all come from?

Throughout the book, I have referred to a "BDEEP." BDEEP (pronounced B-DEEP) is the collection of Beliefs, Definitions, Experiences, Expectations, and Perceptions we each have that define our reality. It literally controls what we think is possible, what we think we can have, and what we believe is outside our access. Here are working definitions for reference.

Beliefs are those things we hold as true or correct. They may be positive beliefs or negative beliefs. We might have a belief about creation, our divine heritage, or the divine world. We certainly have beliefs about our own worth, the behavior and value of others, and where we fit in both the micro and the macro scheme of things.

Definitions are the meanings we assign. Words like love, compassion, forgiveness, opportunity, fairness, justice, and many others form a framework of how we assess and assign meaning to the different experiences we have.

Experiences are events we have personally passed through. Perhaps they were inflicted upon us by the words or actions of others. Perhaps they came from our own actions or inaction. Some are part of our genetics, social milieu, or upbringing. In addition, there are things that happen in the world. Earthquakes, weather incidents, wars, poverty, illness, good fortune, and all the rest. Each of these are stones in the foundation of how we interpret the past and project the future.

Expectations are things that have not yet happened. It is what we expect to happen based on what has happened before, what everything and everyone around us appears to be doing, and what seems reasonable or logical.

Perceptions is the color we give to everything. Because we have a unique genetic makeup and a totally unique set of experiences, how we perceive our lives from moment to moment is different from anyone else. Every conversation you hear. Every act you see or hear about. Every cloud in the sky and thought in your head is interpreted in a particular way based on the life lenses you wear.

Taken together, this entire set of things forms your Context. We generally interpret our context as absolute and certain, even when it is completely uncertain. Our context frames and defines our reality.

This all goes on in the background, and we assume it is reality. Our interpretation of circumstance is not subject to question unless we actively question it. This means such a context often forms a straitjacket that constrains our view of life, our possibilities, what the past means, and what the future holds.

The truth is your context is transparent and flexible, not opaque and ironclad. This discovery is the basis for all change. Since we start with only our own interpretation and the input of others, all filtered through our life lenses, we are extremely limited in our understanding of the real truth in any situation.

This gives rise to massive uncertainty. We think we know something, and yet we always have a feeling there is something we don't know, something we can't understand, and stuff we can't control. Those feelings are real and true.

Past experience dictates we fail. Past experience involves ridicule from peers, strangers, and even family members. Past experience includes judgment where we are shown we are lacking and not good enough in some way.

Past experience may include betrayal from friends, lovers, business partners, and others. We learn that life includes a big dose of getting hurt. We have a very small collection of these memories when we are young. As we get older, we accumulate more and more, and consequently, our level of uncertainty grows and fear multiplies.

This collection creates the quicksand of "The Underneath." That nagging voice in your head that always has the doubt, the fear, the assertion you will fail, the belief you will be embarrassed, and waives the flag of "you better not try."

Unless we become aware of and eliminate the effects of "The Underneath," it plays an increasingly larger role in our daily experience, decision-making, aspirations, and ultimately the entire experience of our lives. In *The Book of Context,* I provide a framework for assessing and changing your context to benefit your growth and prosperity.

Chapter 18

How Does "The Underneath" Show Up?

Everyone is different, so the answer to this question varies. But not as much as you might think. There are common characteristics and effects this quicksand has on daily life and long-term success and joy.

Some examples will illustrate this point. Look at each of these examples and identify parallels in your life. Intentionally make the connections rather than arguing for differences, which justifies the thought, "Yeah, but I'm different."

1. You assess your situation and decide you want more money. You look at your job and the prospects for promotion. You know the people you work with will stab you in the back, and the jerk you work for won't recognize your efforts, so there's not much hope there.
2. You have a wake-up call about your health. You've known for a long time you need to get in better shape and perhaps lose some weight. Immediately, the number of things you've tried and the half-hearted efforts of the past stare you in the face, and you ruefully decide there's just no way to change anything.
3. Someone you know has some good fortune. You want to feel happy for them, but secretly, you feel they are undeserving and wonder why someone else always gets the breaks.
4. You attend a personal development seminar and get excited about a new morning gratitude process to improve your daily experience. You do it for a couple of days; then you

get up late, your commitment wanes, and you believe it wouldn't work for you anyway, so you give up.

5. You hire a coach because a friend of yours has had some good experience with coaching. You hesitate to set clear intentions and find yourself arguing for your limitations. You have nagging doubts that overwhelm your tentative commitment. It doesn't "work," and you berate yourself for being duped and wasting the money.
6. Something happens that reconnects you to a passion you've had for many years. You want to do something with it, perhaps create a side hustle. As soon as you start, obstacles show up, and you doubt your ability to make it happen, so it fades back into the mist of wishing.
7. You notice a pattern in your life of starting things and not finishing. It bothers you a lot, and you secretly feel that somehow you aren't worthy, can't get it together, and don't deserve success anyway. You settle in with the feeling of resignation.
8. You feel cracks and failures in your existing relationship with your life partner. You secretly know that you share some responsibility. Changing anything feels scary, so instead, you focus on the failings of your significant other. After all, if they would just stop doing _______________, you might be inclined to be more involved, caring, intimate, or whatever.

There are dozens more examples. Take some time to list yours. The important point isn't the number of possibilities. It is that you take this opportunity to explore how this feeling of unworthiness, self-sabotage, fear of failure, fear of success, fear of ridicule, and all the other nuances of this expression show up in your life.

Every time your heart speaks, the other voice of doubt, fear, and potential failure shouts so loudly or whispers so persuasively that you give up. Your existing context has prevailed once again and prevented you from moving forward.

The sad and powerful thing about this situation is you genuinely believe the stories about not being good enough.

- That's just how I am.
- It's too late.
- I've already tried all that.
- Everything is stacked against me.
- I have too many obligations.
- It's just too hard.
- I have no support.
- I'll be embarrassed and die.
- And all the other ways of expressing this fear.

The liberating and staggering truth about this situation is that "The Underneath" in all its forms and manifestations only exists in your mind. I don't care what anyone says or does; how you feel about it and how you let it affect you is yours to decide.

Yours alone.

Your life is yours. You may feel you owe it to others, but it is still yours. One hundred percent, all the time, every day, every choice, and every opportunity. Whether you use them or not, the choices and life are yours.

Chapter 19

What Is Bedrock?

In construction, bedrock is the unshakable, solid mass of stone required for big structures to stand firmly through time and natural events.

The "underneath" is the opposite of bedrock. It is shifting sands, uncertainties, and it always feels like it could change in unpredictable ways any minute and bring your whole pile of work crashing around your feet with all the accompanying embarrassment and shame.

You are not building a building, but you are building your life, your relationships with the Divine, with yourself, and with others. You are building a business of value. You are pursuing purpose and meaning in your life. You don't want to build on sand, high-sounding words, or pretend you are something you are not. That structure won't last.

You need bedrock, and if you search, there is bedrock to be found.

I define the ultimate life as a life of Purpose, Prosperity, and Joy built on bedrock. It doesn't come accidentally but as a consequence of your own creation. It is created from a choice to love and serve from your life experience and divine gifts. When it is built on bedrock, it will weather the most difficult external experiences and struggles.

For construction, bedrock is where it is. We don't create the bedrock of the earth. When someone wants to build a significant structure where bedrock is too deep or unavailable, substitutes are created by driving piles deep into the earth. How deep they are driven is determined by the composition of the earth, the geography of the area, and other factors.

In building your life, you choose whether you create bedrock or not. Bedrock is the foundation you build for your life based on intentionally facing and addressing the difficult questions we have asked ourselves for millennia. Since everyone's life experience is completely different, your questions and answers will be your own.

It is not the questions themselves that allow you to form the bedrock for your life. It is the act of formulating and addressing the seemingly unanswerable questions and then making choices for yourself about how you create from your answers.

Here are some questions I used to create a bedrock of certainty and choice for my life.

1. Do I believe in a divine, intentional creation?
2. Is that divine power intentional or accidental?
3. Is that divine power personal, in that it knows me, or is it abstract?
4. Is my belief a certainty, or does it change subject to whatever is going on?
5. Am I willing to allow for the existence of powers greater than me that are intimately involved in my life?
6. Is there such a thing as absolute truth?
7. Is truth available to be known, or is it like the proverbial elephant? It depends on what I'm touching at the time.
8. Am I created for a purpose or just a random event?
9. Do I believe love is the most powerful force, or is it just a nice idea?
10. Are there principles that guide me, that apply in every situation, no matter what?
11. Do I take responsibility for creating my own life, or do I give that responsibility to others, circumstances, and other externalities?

12. Do I want to create a bedrock for myself, or would I rather live in a shifting and relativistic moral interpretation of my world?
13. Am I willing to allow every other person to ask and answer these questions, or not ask them, in any way they choose?

This is by no means a complete list. There are several ways to frame all these questions and other related ideas.

Bedrock is the choice to accept that there are foundational truths about our creation, purpose, and existence we can access, claim, and rely on no matter what else is going on.

If these certainties are variable, then it is like soil that becomes unstable because of liquefaction, seismic action, unexpected and unknown circumstances in the earth, or other reasons.

Creating bedrock for your life is a choice. You will choose it or you won't. You will choose when you do this work. This chapter is titled "What is bedrock?" The simple answer is bedrock is a choice you make about the foundations of your life.

Chapter 20

Creating a Foundation

After you choose whether you wish to create your bedrock, or a solid foundation for your life, and you make a choice about what lines of inquiry are required, you must set about building that foundation.

In choosing a foundation for a building, the process is the same. The decision is made to build a building in a certain place, then the soil is studied, bedrock depth determined, characteristics of the building are decided, and the required calculations are made about loadbearing, seismic activity, water tables, liquefaction, and all the other variables that go into the equation.

In your building, you make choices about founding principles and relevant inquiries needed to answer things you consider important. During your formulation and research into your own heart, you will make adjustments and changes just like you would when doing soil studies. As the work progresses, you make discoveries, determinations, and refinements.

After your internal reflection and choices are complete, you set about building the foundation. Up to then, all you have is some information and knowledge about what would be required to create a foundation based on your specifications and choices.

Building a foundation that will stand the test of time, the unforeseen struggles and circumstances that will undoubtedly occur, and the unfolding experiences of your life is a challenging process. It is not for the faint-hearted. The rewards are infinite.

In building construction, it is common for changes in specifications to occur as the piles for the foundation are driven into the earth. My research showed at least 15 different reasons why the pile driving goes differently than planned and why the foundation must be adjusted.

Buildings are constructed according to laws, seismic standards, and all the other variables associated with geology, soil conditions, and other factors. Even though it is impossible to have a perfect knowledge of all those things, the buildings are completed anyway.

Building foundations are designed to withstand estimated seismic variations, weather impacts, and other forces that may challenge the foundation's integrity. In a similar fashion, your foundation will be built on everything you can know at the time of its construction. You will also build in the ability to change, adjust, and manage your life as external forces challenge your choices.

Building an internal foundation is not about perfection, not about complete enlightenment, and not about being right about everything. It is a set of choices you make on which you build your life, given that you know that life unfolds, things change, you learn new truths, and you gain new perspective.

The other choice is not to build a foundation and simply abdicate because you can't know everything for certain. You end up living in a variable condition based on what's going on at the time and simply do what seems right in the moment without reference to firm internal bedrock.

Without passing any judgment, my observation has been those who live without foundation get tossed around a lot more by the uncertainties of life. Those with a foundation, are happier and offer more service in the world, even when unforeseen tragedies, changes, and other unexpected events overwhelm and even derail the plans they have for life.

In any case, whether you choose to put the time and effort into your foundation is your choice. If you choose to put in the work, how you approach this is also your decision. I'm writing this book to share what I did to create a foundation and to provide ideas for you to create your own.

Because of my experience, I would absolutely encourage you to do the work. As I work with many people, the benefits always outweigh the effort and the uncertainties 100% of the time. I believe it's worth any effort to create your own firm foundation.

Chapter 21

No Permission, No Agreement

The next several chapters assume you decided to create a foundation for yourself. I will share observations from my experience that helped me and those I have served in creating a foundation that is firm, lasting, and insanely motivating.

From early life on, we live in a world of pleasing others. An infant learns to cry to get attention, and then a toddler learns to perform. Learning to walk and getting praise, behaving well sometimes, and misbehaving other times, all succeed in getting attention.

Animals are the same. Every dog I've ever owned always sticks his nose under my hand because he or she wants to be petted. We are social creatures and function best in a harmonious community.

The problems come when we think that we must twist and contort ourselves to gain that attention and approval. This twisted learning process begins at the same time. When we misbehave, we get punished. Though that is attention, soon we lose privileges and don't enjoy the outcome.

As a child and then a young adult navigates the world, getting permission is an integral part of development. You must pass the driver's test to get a driver's license. You must have a certain level of proficiency to graduate from high school or get into university.

Professional licensing exams and everything else follow the same pattern. In selecting a life partner, we follow essentially the same process. There is much about the mating dance that involves getting permission and approval.

There are many negative aspects to this conformity. Kids go to college and get degrees in areas they don't find interesting. People become lawyers and doctors because it was expected. People pursue something other than their dreams and passions because, in their family or culture, the dream or passion is not approved.

I'm not trying to create a bright line that marks the boundary of appropriate conformity. I point these things out because in the process of creating your personal foundation, you need to toss all that out the window and start from scratch.

Undoubtedly, the things you've learned, experienced, come to believe, and enjoy play a part in creating the foundation for your life. It will be critical to observe where your own desires end, and where "What I Think Others Think" (The WITOT Fungus) has infected your existing context.

The truth is you need no one's permission to build the foundation for your life. Others may agree or disagree. Depending on the level of agreement or disagreement, they may cut you out of their lives and never talk to you again.

That makes absolutely no difference unless you let it make a difference. Since we are beginning at the most fundamental, powerful, and basic level of existence, the opinions of others need have no bearing on your thinking. This is as it should be.

At the end of the day, you need to look yourself in the mirror, love exactly who you are and who you are becoming if you want to create motivating Purpose and Power and live your ultimate life. Remember, our starting definition of the ultimate life is a life of purpose, prosperity, and joy that you create with your skills, gifts, and life experience.

I expect that by now, you've already created a starting definition of your ultimate life. It may start tentatively. It must grow to become clear and powerful for you. In these next chapters, anything wishy-washy will not serve you, will not last, and ultimately will serve as a model of what not to do.

In chapter 14, I talked about creating a collection of declarations that define who you are. If you don't have them, this is where we begin that process. If you do have them, look in the mirror and say them out loud to yourself. Whisper them, shout them.

If they don't rattle your bones and light the walls on fire, or make you weep and tremble with both excitement and anticipation, they are not yet worthy as a foundation for an eternal being. You are infinite and eternal, and your declarations should match.

In these exercises, you need no one's permission. No one needs to give you the nod to declare who you are in the world. This is a contract and agreement between you and your creator. Maybe you will share these with others and maybe you won't. The point is they must serve you, inspire you, and be an anchor and a refuge.

In these exercises, you need no one's agreement. If you were to share and someone were to disapprove, that doesn't matter. They have their own lenses through which they see life. Each person could be busy creating their own life purpose instead of minding others' business.

Sometimes, we seek agreement even without talking to others. We imagine what someone might think or say based on hearing the declarations about ourselves. That implied approbation, agreement, or permission is also unnecessary and often harmful.

The next chapters will give you ideas about creating declarations that resonate through you and serve as your starting point. Remember, this will be an iterative process, and will likely change over time as you will evolve and grow.

Nothing happens until you start. The fundamental point is to fully realize you need no one's permission and no one's agreement as you begin this journey. So, start now. Stay with it. This process can change your life.

Chapter 22

What's On a Headstone?

One interesting way to think about making choices and declaring who you are is to answer the question, "If someone were to create a headstone for me right now, and truthfully write on it how others see me, what would they say?"

This is not about creating a glorifying eulogy. It is not remembering only positive things, even though that is what we tend to do. This is just about truth. Perhaps another way to think about this is, "If my friends and colleagues were in honest conversation, and I was not there, how would they describe me?"

"Oh yeah, she's the woman that ________."

"Of course I know him, he's the man who always _________."

Depending on who you are being in the world right now, some words that might come to mind are:

- Always on time.
- Always disorganized.
- Can't be depended on.
- Always has a kind word.
- Usually, self-absorbed.
- Very spiritual.
- Volunteers to help with everything.
- Always has a smile.
- You can't trust them further than you can throw them.
- You never know what you're going to get with them.
- Always has your back.

- Would sell their mother for the right price.
- Always trying to build people up.
- Only in it for themselves.
- Trustworthy, no matter what.

There are hundreds of other possibilities. The idea is to get started on who you've been up to now. Obviously, everyone's opinion is colored through their own lenses. Nevertheless, if complete truth were spoken and nothing was shaded because of cultural norms, what do people actually think?

I'm not suggesting you twist or contort yourself so all the phrases are flattering or good. I am suggesting you tell the truth and see if the collection of things you truly believe others would say, in total honesty, represents the person you want to be in the world.

When I first did this exercise, I was horrified at the list of things I thought people would say. Many were true. I had secrets, I had skeletons, I had behaviors I was not proud of, and the thought of them becoming known scared me to death. The story of my old life and the transformation is in the book *Tightrope of Depression* if you want details.

If this exercise scares you, good. If it wakes a desire in you to create fundamental change, even better. Growth is the natural state of our existence. Equilibrium doesn't exist.

Take some time as you do this exercise. Then, wait a day or two and do it again. Then, wait a day or two and do it again. Notice the correlation between your mood and of the words you might write. Also, notice the correlation between external events that occur right before each iteration and your answers.

This is not an exercise in self-loathing, self-flagellation, or anything like that. It is an opportunity to begin, perhaps for the first time in your life, to not only be honest about who you have been, but about your own desire to create change and take ownership of who you are, moment to moment.

Living a life in absolute peace, with no worry about anything that happens, and being unafraid of who knows what, is an achievable state. It is only achievable if you understand and intentionally create who you are in every moment.

While this might begin fearfully for you, soon, you will reflect on these words with joy. When you realize no matter what has come before, it is never too late to have a big impact and really matter in the world if you make conscious choices and work at it every day.

After you think about what people might say, in a different column, truthfully write down what you want to be true. Hiding and pretending are not allowed. You notice I said what you want to be true and not what you want others to say.

The only thing that matters is what is true, without excuse, without shading, without minimizing, and without aggrandizing. Simply write down the words you want to be true on your headstone or in any description of who you are.

Something that helps me with this is thinking about what the scriptures call "the final judgment." I don't know how it's going to look, but I imagine standing in front of God and going over who I am. I came into the world with nothing except the gifts He gave me, and when I stand there, I will be the person I have made of myself from those gifts and my life experience.

There will be no shading, minimizing, pretending, blaming, or making excuses. What I have made of myself will be completely and totally transparent. Maybe there won't be any words needed. When I think about that moment, it used to scare me to death. I could not imagine appearing in that place with the truth of my being completely exposed.

Today, with the work I have done and following the processes in this book, I have absolutely no fear. I know exactly what will happen. I know exactly who I am in front of the divine. I clearly know every mistake I still make, and every weakness I still have. I also know every effort and commitment I make daily to joyfully grow and add good to the world.

If you shortchange this exercise, it won't do anything for you. If you do it deliciously, carefully, and iteratively, it will give you great rewards and turn out to be something powerful you not only know, but can repeat whenever you feel the desire.

Chapter 23

Start Small

The next two chapters describe a process to create statements to help you fashion your guiding stars. I assume you fully intend to create powerful documents to activate your divine potential, guide your life, and tap into your infinite possibility.

One way to begin creating declarations consistent with your heart's desire is to start small. If you have been plagued by self-doubt, self-loathing, and other forms of negative self-talk, starting with big, bold statements may feel so inauthentic as to be useless.

The documents we create are alive and iterate as often as they need to. Starting small is a way to reduce resistance you might feel to words or phrases you begin to write down. Be sure to write them down. Writing is more memorable than using a computer or just thinking.

In beginning the process of making declarations about who you are, let's remember several things. First, no one is perfect. The act of creating declarations is not a denial of our humanity. Nor is it puffery or pretending to be something we can't achieve.

Second, because we aren't perfect, such declarations are of necessity or aspirational. Start with a vision of yourself in your most glorified, beautiful, and powerful state.

Third, it is important that the declarations are firm and not written with wishy-washy words, or words that invite excuses. No one aiming for a state championship, national title, or the Olympic podium ever said, "Well, I'm going to try to do good, so maybe I can get to the Olympics sometime."

Fourth, because no one needs to agree or give permission, these statements are declared from your deepest heart, your strongest longing, and recognizing you truly are a divine being created with purpose and the opportunity to be anything.

Fifth, sometimes people think because something isn't finished, it is inauthentic to make bold declarations in the present tense. That is not true. It is an authentic, bold, declarative promise. It is uttered from your deepest heart and with every conviction of your soul. There is a world of difference between, "I'm going to try to watch my temper today" and "I will stop and think before speaking, and make certain every word is true and kind."

Sixth, each declaration doesn't need to be grandiose to be effective. The declaration needs to represent a truthful and honest commitment. A commitment you intend to complete not only by speaking it but by structuring your actions so everything that needs to be done is done to bring it to pass.

Here are some examples of small yet powerful declarations to illustrate potential starting points:

- I am that I make a 2% improvement today in the number of sales calls I make.
- I am that I remember to stop and think before I speak at least three times today.
- I am that I do not hit the snooze button one single day this week.
- I am that I look in the mirror and say to myself, "I love you," three days this week.
- I am that I choose to put my partner first when we make joint decisions each day this week.
- I am that I do not exaggerate anything I say for the next 24 hours.

- I am that I laugh the next time something happens I don't expect or want.
- I am that I go three days without swearing at someone.
- I am that I yield in traffic in three situations where I previously would have been aggressive.
- I am that I exercise for 10 minutes on the floor next to the bed, two days this week.
- I am that I express love to my partner two extra times this week.
- I am that I choose to listen to my child until they are finished talking for the next two days.

None of these may have anything to do with your personal needs. I use them because they illustrate the simple yet profound nature of beginning a process of making declarations that you keep sacred and accomplish at all costs.

It is far more important to keep the declarations you make than it is to make grandiose statements. This is especially true when you have either failed before or are likely to fail in the present.

This may be a new way of speaking to yourself, setting goals, or creating your own being. If it's new for you, good. It is powerful. However, it won't do anything if you don't practice.

The point is to make a declaration. An affirmative statement you treat as written in fire and steel in your heart, and on the walls of the universe. It is not negotiable; it is truth. It simply IS.

If you are in the habit of making promises to yourself and breaking them, starting small is essential. Repeating the old process of making big promises and failing ensures continued failure. You teach yourself you can't be trusted, and nothing will change.

You need a new system. So, make the declarations small enough that with real effort, you can make them happen consistently and without exception. Using this approach, you teach yourself a new truth. You can be trusted.

The goal of this book is to help you purposely create yourself in a way you love. It is to create yourself so you are exactly as you wish to be, have nothing to hide, and nothing to be ashamed of. No skeletons in the closet, no camouflage, duplicity, or guile.

When that condition is the truth of your being, your life is peaceful, and there is nothing you cannot do, nothing you cannot face, and your opportunity to create is infinite. Because this is new for most people, starting small is a guaranteed way to create initial success.

This part of the book will help you with "Creating Your Guiding Star." Starting with declarations small enough that you can guarantee success, gives you certainty in your ability to change and power to move forward and succeed at much bolder declarations.

Chapter 24

Start Outrageously

Starting with small declarations can guarantee initial success. It is not the only place you can start. You may want to start in two places at the same time.

In creating declarations about your being, and who you choose to be in the world, there are a few more things to remember besides those listed in chapter 23. First, you are a divine being. You were created intentionally by the creator of all things.

No matter what your spiritual inclinations are, or what religion you do or don't practice, it is a simple truth: you were created by the same God that created me and everything else. Whatever name or description you give to that infinite power, it is still the source of your creation.

Second, because you are a divine being, there is nothing outside your reach. A peach has a seed in it that grows up to be a peach tree and produces wonderful fruit. Each creation carries in it the seeds to grow and then become exactly like the tree or source from which it sprang.

Third, we have constructed a world where failure is expected, mediocrity is the norm, minimization of others is a regular practice, and we are brainwashed by multiple sources that there are few "exceptional people." The rest of us must settle for what is easy and obvious.

This is false and harmful. Each person came from the same source and has the same opportunities. Obviously, geographical differences, economic differences, family situation differences, physical challenges, and a host of other things present each person with a different playing field.

Nevertheless, you have the ability to use your existing skills, natural gifts, life experiences, and declarations to create anything you want, starting from wherever you are. You can make excuses about why this can't happen, or you can lean in and cause it to BE.

Here are some examples of bold and far-reaching declarations you might make:

- I am forgiveness. I hold no judgment toward anyone.
- I am honesty. I speak only truth.
- I am compassion. I act from love and kindness.
- I am infinitely creative.
- I am that I never give up. I always find a way forward.
- I am that I listen to each person fully and with love.
- I am the infinite universe.
- I am a divine being with infinite potential.
- I am that I create extraordinary wealth and use it to add good to the world.
- I am that I write powerful books that change lives.
- I am that I treat my body as a temple, both physically and spiritually.
- I am that I intentionally study and grow to absorb more eternal truth.
- I am that I live to serve.
- I am that I stand for those with no voice and create a safe place for them to be.

Some of these may speak to you. Or, they may have nothing to do with who you desire yourself to be. This is an example of bigger or more far-reaching declarations you could make about your being.

I am giving these examples as an invitation to create your own. Write down the most outrageous statements that resonate with your deepest heart and cause you to tremble with excitement and possibility.

Since you're doing this by yourself, for yourself, there are no judgments except those you allow in your mind and heart. Set those on the shelf for the moment. They are nothing but an accumulation of old stories. Take all the time you need to play with these declarations until you begin to understand their purpose and invincible power.

It's easy to look at such grandiose statements and become intimidated or feel they are false. No one is perfect, but you are growing. Powerful, declarative, aspirational, fire-breathing commitments are the substance of real growth.

Those who first climbed Mount Everest started with declarative statements they would make this ascent and reach the summit. Sometimes, initial failure intervened, but the invincible primordial declaration eventually came into being.

To achieve anything of substance in life, you must first picture it in your mind and then declare an unalterable commitment to get there. You could say, "I'm going to keep trying until this or that happens." That is weak and does not evoke powerful creative energy.

"I am that I accomplish that goal, regardless of detours, resistance, and setbacks." That declaration carries more power, is more inspirational, and creates a more motivating vision.

In these two chapters, I have talked about starting with both small and outrageous declarations. You may want to do both. They serve different functions.

Small declarations create the evidence you can trust yourself and know you can speak your reality into existence. You speak a thing and then cause it to happen. Starting small enough that this pattern becomes your state of being is a powerful way to learn to apply this skill.

Outrageous declarations create a vision of who you truly are and what is available to you. Dream outrageously. Whisper them. Scream them. Write them down. Record them. Listen to them in your own voice over and over. Live the truth of them until it radiates fire in every molecule of your body.

Remember, you need no one's permission and no one's agreement. You only need your committed choice to be and live into the truth of your divine heritage and infinite possibility.

Chapter 25

Declarations vs. Affirmations

A popular practice in positive psychology is creating so-called affirmations. This chapter addresses the difference between affirmations and declarations and explains why affirmations may be useful but are a watered-down substitute with less power than soul-stirring declarations.

For those who may use affirmations in their daily practice now, I do not intend to offend. I am introducing you to an exponentially more powerful approach to speed your growth and feed your soul.

One of the most famous affirmations was, "Every day, in every way, I am getting better and better." This was first used by Emile Coue in connection with medication. He noticed praising the effectiveness of medication increased its effectiveness. There are hundreds, if not thousands, of other affirmations I have heard, used myself, and seen others use.

I have clients who have documents written at seminars with lists of these affirmations. When I begin this work with clients, they often dig into their computer or a binder and pull out a statement they crafted a month, a year, or even ten years ago.

When I ask if their statement is memorized, they usually say no. Then I ask if they use the statements every day to create their lives, handle both positive and challenging circumstances, and enter into the world exactly as they choose. The answer is usually "no" or "occasionally."

Then I ask if reciting the document creates unshakable fire and power in their souls. The answer is always "no." Often, they don't believe such a statement can create world-changing power. That is not surprising because they have never created such a declaration.

There is no doubt choosing optimism and speaking positively to yourself or others is a beneficial choice and a good habit to create. Speaking growth-based words instead of catastrophizing every circumstance helps with creativity, resilience, and finding solutions to everyday problems.

Affirmations are often statements about yourself and your life you don't believe about yourself but wish were true. They usually consist of attitudes and characteristics you want to be real but are usually not paired with any intentional focused effort to create those attributes.

Repeated repetition is an effort to talk yourself into something you don't believe. This is not very effective because all of this work takes place on top of the shifting sands of "The Underneath."

There is no foundation for the affirmation other than the wish you have for it to be true. As you speak affirmations, often doubts and fears swirl in the quicksand under your feet. That feeling undermines their power in the very moment of speaking.

This is particularly true in difficult situations when you are trying to create a reaction that is empowering, after something unexpected and perhaps difficult has happened. Repeating affirmations while fear grips your stomach and uncertainty clouds your judgment and creativity might create a momentary sense of calm, but it does little to anchor your soul to the bedrock.

Declarations, when prepared and used as described so far and further strengthened by the following chapters, are connected to the bedrock of eternal truth. They are foundations instead of declarations.

Though they are aspirational in the sense we are not perfect, that fact does not change the absolute clarity and resoluteness of your determination to be the things you have declared yourself to be.

That is why it is critical to prepare declarations founded on your deepest beliefs, unfettered and undiluted by the voices of doubt and fear from past experience and other elements of your context or BDEEP (Beliefs, Definitions, Experiences, Expectations, and Perceptions.)

This is why declarations begin with I AM. Some declarations are simply acknowledgments of eternal truth and cannot be questioned. "I AM a divine creation" is not aspirational. It is a statement of fact about how you came into being. Some declarations are aspirational, such as "I AM My Word and Speak Only Truth." That may be a work in progress, but when done properly, it is intensely motivating and transformational.

Since you choose your beliefs, there can be no argument with any declaration. You choose what you believe. You choose how you express it. You declare your belief. You declare your commitment. You choose what you do if you fall or fail in any declaration.

The beliefs that come in the BDEEP are those created by old experiences and things others have said that you have allowed to influence who you are at present. They can be deep and powerful but are still only yours if you allow it.

Affirmations are often spoken rapidly, repeatedly, and sometimes almost mindlessly, hoping by continued repetition to talk you into something you wish for but don't believe.

Declarations are spoken deliberately and forcefully with the intention of igniting the fire of truth, stirring the power of deep belief, and magnifying the love and creativity we all have, even though, at times, it may feel distant and inaccessible.

In creating your guiding star, the goal and the outcome is to create vibrant, powerful, and soul-stirring words you own in that deep inner chamber, words you truly believe in, and words that set your heart aflame every time you read them.

I often say to clients, "If your statement doesn't make you weep every time you read it, write it again."

Chapter 26

Explanation of Documents

When we think about getting a big project completed, we generally ask two questions. First, "What am I going to accomplish?" This includes precise descriptions of the desired outcome, deadlines we create or accept, and milestones to measure progress.

Second, we ask, "How will we accomplish this thing?" This includes time required, knowledge, skills, resources, money, people, and anything else we think we need to get it done.

While this is obvious when you think about large external projects, the same is true about creating your life, moment-to-moment, and day-to-day. If you don't have plans for the day, the week, or the year, what you get done will likely be haphazard and scattered.

There are thousands of books about how to get things done. The entire discipline of project management focuses on this activity. I wrote *The Results Equation – From Dream to Done in Five Simple Steps* as another take on a powerful way to get goals accomplished.

There is something dramatic missing from the normal "outside-in" approach. This missing element is usually ignored, glossed over, or assumed away. It is left out because it is difficult to define and perceived as less tangible.

Yet the missing piece is more powerful than all the other elements combined. It is the most important question of all and should be asked and answered definitively. This is especially true when we are creating the outcomes of our lives.

The question is this: "Who do you need to be to create this project?" This question applies to every minute of your life. It is the determinative factor in how well the first two questions work. There are many versions of this question. Here are a few:

- Who are you going to be as you create your day?
- Who are you going to be as you create your relationships?
- Who are you going to be as you go to work?
- Who are you going to be as you build your business?
- Who are you going to be as you interact with every person you think about, pray about, talk to, work with, or avoid?
- Who are you going to be as you relate to your creator?
- Who are you going to be as you examine your habits and practices and decide to stay the same or change?

This is the same question over and over again. It sends us back to where we started at the beginning of the book: "Who are YOU?" We ignore this question too much, even though it impacts everything we do.

Creating living and powerful documents is the work of considering, choosing, and using your chosen answer to this eternally significant, ultimately profound, life-defining question. The answer, whether created accidentally or intentionally, drives every moment and experience of your existence.

I have worked for years creating the documents that guide my life. I share them with you here as an example of one person's outcome of this process. I share them by way of illustration to give you an idea of what might be created.

These documents are mine. They are intended to help me define and be who I choose. Sharing them is the ultimate vulnerability. My intent and sincere hope is that they are useful for you, both to encourage you to create your own and to help you understand you need no one's permission or agreement to create your destiny.

Next is a diagram with the names and descriptions of the three main documents I use.

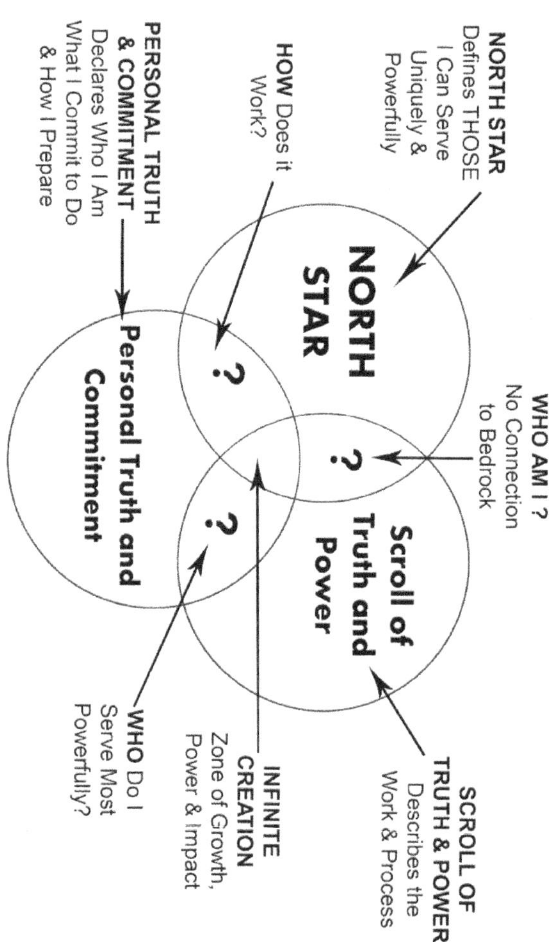
NORTH STAR
Defines THOSE
I Can Serve
Uniquely &
Powerfully
WHO AM I ?
No Connection
to Bedrock
SCROLL OF
TRUTH & POWER
Describes the
Work & Process
HOW Does it
Work?
NORTH
STAR
?
?
Scroll of
Truth and
Power
INFINITE
CREATION
Zone of Growth,
Power & Impact
PERSONAL TRUTH
& COMMITMENT
Declares Who I Am
What I Commit to Do
& How I Prepare
Personal Truth and
Commitment
?
WHO Do I
Serve Most
Powerfully?

The first and foundation document is the PTAC: "Personal Truth and Commitment." It declares who I AM. It also declares my relationship to God, the universe, others, and myself. Some declarations are factual statements to remind me of my origin. Some are aspirational and declare the intentional direction and outcome of my life journey.

The PTAC also declares the work I choose for myself. It declares how I do that work and why. It also declares how I prepare myself every day for the purpose and mission I have declared. It is written in the most powerful language I can find, and it is the foundational truth to my soul.

I have it memorized and use it every day. First in the morning to remind me who I am and create my attitude and focus. I use it again during the day any time I have decisions to make or feel my energy or focus waning. Sometimes I whisper. Sometimes I use it as a meditation. Sometimes I shout it to the skies. I have recorded it and listen as I take a walk. It is intentionally woven into the fabric of my being.

This is a choice. I choose to create myself with these words and in this fashion. I choose to use it to define my soul, my commitments, and my purpose in this world. Every time I use it, it lights up my heart, lights fire to the walls, and ignites the deepest chambers of my spirit.

In the book *Tightrope of Depression,* I described my decades-long battle with depression, self-loathing, self-sabotage, addictions, failed relationships, suicide attempts, and many other dark chapters. I described the divine intervention in August and September of 2007 which was the invitation to change.

What most people don't understand, is that even though dramatic interventions, earthly or divine, may smack you on the side of the head, they don't do the work of change. They are a wake-up call, an invitation, a stark reminder, and a glaring spotlight on the realities of the present.

The invitations do not do the work of change.

In the 16 years since that took place, I had to do the work. I found the help, created the relationship with the divine, bared my soul in previously unthinkable ways, and relentlessly pursued the path of change and growth.

The two most important and powerful things I have done in this incredible journey from darkness, despair, and death to light, love, and life are these: first, the creation of these documents. They are living documents. I breathe them. They are woven into my DNA, the fabric of my soul, and written with fire and steel on the walls of my heart.

The second, and perhaps even more important than the first, is the creation of a daily process to remind, ignite, and direct the application of my declarations every day. Without this direction and daily reinforcement, we forget. Even raging emotion and intention gets watered down unless the fire is continually refreshed.

The entire third section of the book will reveal my daily creation process and how I intentionally make every day count by using my guiding stars, by living in the present, and by loving what is.

The second document in the diagram is the North Star. I use that name because of the history the North Star has in the northern hemisphere as a navigational aid. It serves the same function for me. It guides the work I do every minute, of every hour, of every day, in the direction I have chosen and declared. It is also a living document and can be adjusted as needed.

The purpose of the North Star is to declare who I serve. In the PTAC, I state, "I AM that I live to Serve." I cannot serve every person in the world. Each of us resonates more with some than others. Each of us has natural gifts, developed skills, and life experience. These three elements create your unique voice.

My unique voice speaks particularly well to some groups of people. The North Star is my description of those I serve best. This is derived from my experience and by noticing which people are attracted to my tribe. It is the group I seem to impact the most. This is not just to describe who I work with in business but reminds me who I best serve in any circumstance.

Every person has a set of natural gifts, existing skills, and life experience. That unique combination for you constitutes your voice. Using your voice intentionally and powerfully is the path for you to create the most impact, have the most fun, and create the most prosperity in your life.

In the forthcoming book *Masterpiece – Living in Flow and Manifesting Your Creative Genius,* I describe a process for discovering your natural gifts and combining them with your existing skills and life story to create that unique voice as your powerful tool to add good to the world.

The third document is The Scroll of Truth and Power. As you will see, it is intentionally written in script that might appear on an ancient scroll. I imagine in my mind a robed figure holding this scroll majestically and the words being powerfully intoned so they echo off the walls of the chamber and reverberate through the hearts of the hearers.

This document describes the process of growth. Using my own road as an example, I talk about the challenges, temptations, struggles, and victories that occur along the road of development.

I use it to help people see a picture of the epic nature of the task they have chosen for themselves when they embark on the journey of discovering their own awesome capability and turning that infinite resource into an amazing reality in the world.

In the diagram, you see there are three areas where only two of the circles overlap. In each of those areas, the full power of the framework does not come into play. In each area where one element is missing, I describe the consequence of the missing element of the framework.

As I said in the beginning, I share these documents and this framework as an example. It is an illustration of a possibility. It is meaningful to me because I created it and use it powerfully. Please take the time, introspection, and work to create your own declarations.

Craft your own relationship with the Divine, with yourself, with those you serve, and with the rest of the world. Boldly decide who you are and document it in the form that serves you best. What will not serve you is to take a look at this and shrug it off as "an interesting idea." It means nothing at all unless you make a choice and take the effort to make it mean something for you.

You are a divine creation. You have all the characteristics of your divine heritage. You have infinite potential and limitless possibilities. We live in a world that suppresses creativity. We have created a society that stomps on aspiration even as it pretends to glorify those who defy the norm.

Your opportunity is to take these examples and create your own documents to light your soul on fire. Use the most powerful language you can find. Get all the help you can so the shackles of fear, past experience, and outside influence are eliminated.

Boldly discard the voices and fears in your heart and create from the depths of eternity.

Besides the three main documents, I included a few others. These are mainly groupings and restatements of the three primary documents. I created them because it helps me and those I serve, to organize the principles and declarations in different ways and with slightly different language.

They are self-explanatory and included for reference.

Chapter 27

The Documents

Here are the documents I described in the previous chapter and illustrated in the diagram. The first document is my PTAC or Personal Truth and Commitment. I offer no further explanation since it says what it says and is included for your reference and information.

The goal is to help you create your own document, in whatever form and language serves you and lights every cell of your life on fire.

The second document is my North Star. It lays out the description of the people I help most effectively. It describes clients for my business and reminds me of those with whom I have the most resonance.

A deep connection allows me to serve them in whatever capacity is possible given the circumstance, the time we have together, and their individual state of willingness to explore possibilities.

The third document is The Scroll of Truth and Power. It is written in script because that visual represents an ancient scroll full of hidden meaning and magic. This increases its power and resonance.

Formulate your documents in any format and structure you want. Draw pictures, use photos, use colors and whatever creative expression captures the intent of your heart and lights your soul on fire.

The Scroll describes the process I followed, and clients navigate as they explore their divine nature to create and execute their chosen life purpose. It is a guide since I don't pretend to decide what any individual needs to do.

My work is to help you understand you have infinite power and that exercising your sovereign right to choose and create is the path to purpose, prosperity, and joy. When you combine your existing skills, natural gifts, and unique life experiences, you become a voice that is powerful, influential, and fulfilling.

The other documents are different formulations of the same principles for other purposes and are self-explanatory.

Being

I AM Infinite and Eternal.
I AM a son of Almighty God.
I AM a disciple and friend of Jesus Christ.
I AM at Cause.
(I Create my being and call into existence every part of my experience.)
I AM Love (and pour over your soul like warm sunshine.)
I AM Forgiveness.
(Holding no judgement, anger, or loathing toward anyone for anything, including myself.)
I AM My Word.
(I Speak Only Truth. I Do What I Say. I Am Who I Seem,
with no Camouflage, Duplicity or Guile.)
I AM that I love Joy with Everything that I AM.
Joy is the love of my life and eternity.
I love the grace, beauty, and brilliance that is Joy with all my being.
Joy is my song, my balance, and the light in my heart.
I AM that I have no internal conflict.
I AM that I have no withholding in my being.
I AM the Voice.
(I Tell Stories of Transformation, Sing Songs of Inspiration,
and Speak Words of Power, to help You see Who You Really Are
and Create from Your Infinite Possibility.)
I AM Music (and write songs with Lyrics of Love and Melody of Magic.)
I AM Flow (Love and Truth flow through me, creating words
and works of meaning and value, so miracles appear.)
I AM that I live to work as an instrument in Divine Hands
(with no desire for glory or fear of humiliation.)
I AM Light (and invite you home to yourself.)
I AM Fire (and infuse your heart with courage.)
I AM that I Live Fully Present in Each Moment,
Guided by Spirit, Free, Unattached, and Loving What Is.
I AM that every Imagination I See and every Desire I Dream
is Manifest as I Add Good to The World. and

Love. Create. Serve.

I AM that I Drink Love from Five Fountains:

- **My Creator,** who upholds me and ordains triumph,
- **My Savior,** who leads me, lifts me, and coaches me,
- **The Universe,** which conspires for my good,
- **My Companion,** who walks beside me, encourages me, coaches me,
- **My Self,** with compassion and commitment.

I AM that I love you without hesitation.

- I listen to you fully and without expectation.
- I behold your divine nature and gifts with awe and wonder.
- I acknowledge and serve you, right here, right now.

Overflowing with Love,

- I am **"All In"** loving my God. (He gave me all this and rejoices in my growth.)
- I am **the Knowing** of the Universe.
- I am **Compassion**, (acting in empathy, encouragement, and kindness.)
- I am **Presence**, (radiating Divine power.)
- I am **Open**, (expecting and extracting growth from each experience.)
- I am **Fearless**, (acting in faith and inspiration.)
- I am **Focused**, (walking only the divine path.)
- I am **Committed,** (because I speak it.)
- I am **Gratitude,** (being healed by Divine love.)
- I am **Peace,** (that comes from Unconditional Surrender.)
- I am **Perpetual Joy,** (because I see eternity.)
- I am **GEP,** (Grace, Ease, and Power fueled by Pure Love.)
- I am **Abundance**, (creating infinite expansion – reaching 250MM by Oct. 2024
- and building a 100MM company by Oct. 2025.)
- I am that when I fall or fail in any declaration, I get up, fess up, clean it up, and recommit.

Refined in the Crucible of Trial and Transformed by Love, I Am Become Alchemy

Lover of People, Healer of Souls, Magnifier of Prosperity

I Am Called Kellan

Creating

I AM that I take God's work for my own and joyfully bring souls to Christ (Love) as I become what He intends.

I AM that I have nothing to prove and everything to give.

I AM that I create an encouraging, inclusive, and loving space to listen to you as you've never been heard and see you in your power and possibility. Pure love is the catalyst for growth and change.

I AM that I help you elevate the substance, success, and sweetness of life's journey: By Daring more greatly, Experiencing more deeply, and Leaning-In more joyously.

I AM that I share frameworks and tools that melt barriers, move mountains, and mobilize superpowers to eliminate fear, obliterate doubt, and help you be who you imagine.

I AM that working in empathy, love, and truth, we create your future; however miraculous the work may appear, as we Co-create a vision, Build a path, and Activate required resources.

I AM that I stand for and with you, to help you Love and Serve as you Discover, Develop, and Create from your Life Experience/Divine Gifts.

I AM that every intent is focused, and every action spent to access God's power, complete His mission, and give all praise to God.
To access God's power, I learn about Christ, (He in whose hands the Father hath placed all things,) choose to have faith in Him, make and keep sacred covenants with precision, seeking ways to be unspotted from the world, and reach up to Him in faith (like a drowning man grasping and gasping for air,) because the greatest desire of my heart is to draw His power into my life so I am led by the Holy Ghost to know exactly what to do, and to stretch spiritually more than I have ever done before so His power will flow into me.

I AM that my highest development and greatest joy come in pursuing this path with courage, meekness and unwearyingness.
Meekness is Willing Submissiveness, Righteous Responsiveness and Strong Self-Restraint.

Preparing

I AM that *Every Day I draw Breath I prepare powerfully for the Purpose and Mission I declare.*

I AM that I Pray from my deepest heart to pour out Gratitude; to beg Forgiveness; and to plead for Direction.
I AM that I Listen Intently for Thoughts and Feelings that come during Prayer and throughout the day.
I AM that I Act Without Fear or Delay on Revelation and Answers I receive.

I AM that I Study, Learn from, and Get Coached by Sacred Words:
From the Scriptures,
From the Oracles of God,
From my Companion, Friend, and Helpmeet,
From direct Revelation, especially in the Temple, and
From EACH person in my path, regardless of their standing (rich or poor,) stature (old or young,) or status (famous or unknown.)

I AM that I Care for my Heart and Soul.
I AM that I Look to God in EVERY thought, No Doubt, No Fear.
I AM that I Love and Grow together with my Soulmate.
I AM that I Expand Continuously with Celestial Energy.

I AM that I Care for the Temple that is my Body.
I AM that I Eat well for health and enjoyment.
I AM that I Exercise often for health and strength.
I AM that I Sleep enough for rest and rejuvenation.
I AM that I Heal and Develop through Celestial Energy.

I AM that I Prepare for Clients and Other Service.
I AM that I Consume Uplifting Content in all forms to Stay Sharp.
I AM that I Enter Every Conversation Empty and Listening.
I AM that I Always Remove Ego and Want and Be Pure Love.

North Star

I am the Ultimate Catalyst for
Personal Transformation.

In practical expression, I provide energy, example,
encouragement, and 'permission'
to those ending addiction to mediocrity.

Especially souls with massive hardballs from life
thrown in the mix,
who will not be defined or limited by those things.

These few are done settling
and ready to create big things,
as only they define them.

These commit to live powerfully,
instead of with the obvious or easy.

These choose no matter what,
to discover, develop, and serve with their
Chosen Purpose, Divine Gifts, and Life Experience.

These are driven to be extraordinary:
as parents, leaders, business owners, entrepreneurs,
authors, artists, visionaries, and individuals.

I am that catalyst.

The Scroll of Truth and Power

Stave the First

Guided and Nurtured by God through the Valley of Death and
Refined in Fires of Abuse, Addiction, Depression, and Self-Loathing,
I Am become Alchemy:
Lover of People, Healer of Souls, Magnifier of Prosperity.

Stave the Second

I Create the Space and guide You to Create the Elixir to Transmute the Fury of Injustice, the Ravages of Adversity and the Pain of Loneliness into the Pure Gold of Love, Forgiveness, and Service.

I Am the Catalyst to help You Break the Cage of Doubt, Fear, Loneliness, and Self-Sabotage.

With your Elixir and your Icons of Power, we Face the Fire and Do the Sacred Work to purify Your heart and mind to Become what You alone Define and Declare.

In this Crucible, you Create Yourself. You fashion who you will BE in the world from your Life Experience, and your Divine Nature and Gifts.

Your choices of daily Thoughts and Actions forge the Being You will present to your Creator when your Journey is complete.

Stave the Third

In your Journey, many things may lure or drag you to the Gates of Growth:

- Curiosity,
- Greed,
- Rumours of Riches and Power,
- "They" said you Should,
- It is Expected,
- Pain or Haphazard Circumstance
- Perhaps you feel the Divine Summoning.

At the Gates you look across the Field of Trial and see the Prize in the Distance. You Hear the shrill Voices of Doubt and the Whisper of Encouragement.

At the Gates, many gaze with a Wistful Heart, seeking the Glories of Growth and the Prize of Fulfillment.

Sadly, most souls are not Prepared for the Choices, Sacrifice, and Work Required to Access the Possibility of their Destiny.

Most settle for crumbs. If they engage at all, it is a sad song of Desperately Struggling with overwhelming conflicts they seem Destined to Lose, instead of Courageously Facing developmental challenges they are Determined to Win.

Stave the Fourth

You know you are ready when you see these Signs:

- You choose Meaning and Purpose for your daily life,
- though you sometimes feel it is Beyond your Reach.
- You hold your Vision sacred, though you have been hurt and disappointed.
- You know no one can do your Work and create your Mark in the World.
- You are Fiercely Determined to reach your True Potential,
- regardless of the Work Required or the nameless Fear that Threatens.
- You take Full Responsibility for your Life and no longer blame Others or Circumstance.
- You See yourself in the Mirror of Truth without Judgement or Excuse, and Build with Love from where you are at this Moment.

Stave the Fifth

With these Certainties, you are Prepared for the Quest:

- You create your Icons of Power and Declaration of Being as your Guiding Star.
- You live into that Truth with all your soul,
- Overcoming errors, Learning from setbacks, and Embracing trials.
- You believe Growth responds to Love, Compassion, Invitation, and Effort.
- You learn Growth is hindered by Excuses and Blaming.
- You fiercely own your Life, complete your Commitments, and serve
- with Empathy and Love.
- You boldly continue and Create anything you Desire.
- You know no one can keep you from Living your Truth.

My Mission Statement…

I came into the world to do the will of my Father because I love and trust God with my whole being. My Father's will for me is:

1. ***To Learn*** from my Own Experience and Add Good to the World.

2. ***To Live*** each day as a beacon of LIGHT, a vessel of LOVE and a conduit of POWER, with nothing to prove and everything to give.

3. ***To Love*** you freely and elevate the substance, success, and sweetness of life's amazing journey.

4. ***To Create*** inspired works that come through me to help you Choose Your Purpose, Develop Your Gifts, and Serve Joyfully with all your Being.

5. ***To Be*** the Catalyst for Meaning, Legacy, and Joy to Invite You to Your Highest Self. (Joy is a Choice. The Meaning of Something is the Difference it Makes. If it Makes NO Difference, It Has NO Meaning.)

6. ***To Show*** that no matter what has come before, it is never too late to matter and have big impact as you serve with your Chosen Purpose.

7. ***To Coach*** as my authentic expression of our common Divinity:

- *Because we all share the feeling of inadequacy and the yearning to matter,*
- *Because we deeply desire to Serve and deeply fear Judgement and Rejection,*
- *Because our connectedness in love is strength, and*
- *Because we are anxious to give and receive love.*

Business Plan…

LOVE you with no judgment, as you are
in this moment.
HERE. NOW,
CREATE Space for Imagination to
Blossom and
Creativity to Explode,
SERVE You Fearlessly and in Your
Highest and Best Interest.
I never look for clients. I look for
People to Love, Opportunities to Serve
and Problems to Solve.

Seize the Day...

The Secret to Live In Flow and Cause Miracles to Appear

1. ***Enter*** Spirit and receive pure power.
2. ***Seek*** Inspiration in silence and stillness.
3. ***Speak*** the words of Being to channel power to Love. Create. Serve.
4. ***Affirm*** commitments and eliminate obligations.
5. ***Transform*** negative rumination or interaction.
6. ***Ignore*** irrelevant or distracting thought creations, (imaginary or tangible.)
7. ***Set*** clear measurable commitments.
8. ***Take*** direct consistent motivated action to complete commitments.
9. ***Move*** boldly through the day with focus and creative power.
10. ***Brook*** no internal nonsense.
11. ***Remain*** absorbed each moment in pure service.
    (Like a scene from Frozen, where she waves her hand, and the ice castle appears - let it flow.)
12. ***Manifest*** with boundless joy.

To "Live In Flow and Cause Miracles to Appear," is not a fanciful wish.

It is a declaration and acknowledgement of what happens; when plugged into the infinite power of "Mind;" and using the creative play dough of "Thought;" I create energies, circumstances, and realities that did not previously exist.

Those unfamiliar with the instantaneous and limitless generative nature of "thought-projection," and "mind-energy creation," perceive such manifestations of thoughts, feelings, energies, or physical objects to be outside the realm of the possible - a "miracle."

Helping people grasp and express their own ability to do the same, with their divine heritage and infinite potential, is the ultimate gift.

Part III

Making Every Day Count, Right Here, Right Now

All this would be fun and interesting information but useless in the day-to-day struggle that shows up in every moment and with every breath, unless you take it to ground and use it on demand, on purpose, and with great effect.

Part one of the book demonstrated both the power and process of living in the present moment and loving what is, exactly as it is, as the stance of power for creation.

We live in the present because it is all we have. When we plan for the future and execute that plan, it is by taking action in a successive string of present moments. Living in the present moment does not mean neglecting mistakes or problems of the past, nor does it mean ignoring or failing to plan for the future.

Instead, it exponentially magnifies our ability to do both, by dropping the drama associated with worrying about the past and acting to fix whatever was broken. It also exponentially magnifies our ability to create the future by focusing on present opportunities instead of fearing that goals won't materialize.

Loving what is creates similar benefits. When we live in resistance to what is, we are blinded and unable to take the most effective actions. If we simply acquiesce to what is, we are spared the corrosive effects of negativity, but live in a victim state of hoping instead of creating.

Part II guided you to articulate and commit to whatever principles speak to you in terms of guiding your life, creating your existence, and walking through the world as you choose.

With these things in place, we have the opportunity, if we choose to use it, to be infinitely powerful creators in the present, every moment of every day.

This energy is not frantic busyness. It doesn't preclude excellent and joyful relaxation. It doesn't get in the way of fully enjoying life. On the contrary, it increases our ability to do all these things because we are free from baggage and focused on the present, while armed with clear, self-chosen direction about how we conduct our lives.

This section focuses on the choices we have about how to create every single day. I said earlier that creating the documents was the first of two things most fundamental in reforming my life from darkness, despair, and death, to wild joy and success.

Part III fully shares the second thing that allows me to live every day with purpose, prosperity, and joy. I love every minute of life, live fully in the present and have infinite opportunity.

As with Part II, I will share what I do in my daily process to achieve this result. I do not pretend to tell you how to create this result for yourself. I'm sharing what I do as an example and possibility. I also hope it provides encouragement to take your own documents created in Part II and make them live and breathe as your daily feast.

You can create excuses, or you can create results. Whatever you create, you live with. As you go through each chapter in Part III, please see yourself in every thought, story, and suggestion.

Ask yourself, "How could this benefit my life?" Inquire deeply within what your version of this idea looks like. This work creates freedom, a sense of expansive time, infinite possibility, and unlimited power.

It is interesting that people I work with often talk about a lack of time. Every person breathing air has exactly the same amount of time.

No one has one minute more or one minute lesson in a given day. You have time. You choose every moment how you use it.

Choose creation over consternation. We create life moment-to-moment, whether we do it intentionally or accidentally. Start this moment creating intentionally, just because you can. You are a divine being with infinite capability, so choose your creation intentionally and carefully.

My own practices clearly reveal my spiritual inclinations and beliefs. I make no attempt to decide for you or instruct you on how you should approach the infinite that surrounds us. Whatever you decide to do, do it on purpose, do it full out, and create miracles.

Chapter 28

Why Does It Matter?

After reading the opening section of Part III, you might wonder: "Why all the fuss, I mean, can't I just live day to day and do whatever I feel like?" The answer is simple. You can, and in fact you are living exactly that way right now. You are doing whatever you feel like.

Most people live in the illusion they can't do whatever they feel like. They believe they are somehow constrained by others' wishes, obligations they created for themselves and now resent, and whatever random externalities force them to do.

Those constraints only exist in your mind. You would rather follow those imaginary rules and deny yourself what you want at this moment than do what you want and receive whatever consequences flow from that action. You have beliefs about a set of consequences you allow to limit your choices.

There is no question every action has consequences, but you still choose.

Have you even identified what you truly and passionately want in this moment? Or are you governed by a vague wish list of circumstances powered by longing feelings that have no substance?

Every action is an act of creation. Every thought is an act of creation. Thoughts create feelings, which then create actions, which then produce habits, which lead to our being-ness, which ends up creating our entire lives.

This is not philosophical gibberish. It is the foundational truth of the universe, though most live in either willful or accidental ignorance of this divine truth. You are already doing exactly what you want. You weigh all the factors and imagined outcomes of every choice, and you make your choices based on what you want.

The struggle is the imagined constraints. When you energetically live somewhere besides the present moment, a great deal of energy is wasted on things you can't control right now. When you resist reality, more energy is wasted on things you can't control.

Your creative potential increases exponentially when you drop all those struggles and recapture all that energy. Creating the life of your dreams is easier than you think. There are only three parts.

1. Get really clear about exactly what you want.
2. Create a state of being that aligns with that desire.
3. Take continuous and focused action until the dream is real.

The struggle always seems to be a choice to daydream instead of creating a motivating vision of a future reality. The daydream comes tinged with all the reasons it can't happen, all the excuses about the past, and all the blame about circumstances and others' behavior.

The exercises in Part I and Part II were not provided, so you go through some philosophical work to make bold statements and feel good about your effort. They are intended to arm you with an understanding of unchangeable eternal truth that already exists and help you choose for yourself to create a bedrock from which you live day to day.

Most people never examine their foundational beliefs. Most people live on top of "The Underneath" with the shifting sands, vague fears, and all the baggage that keeps them stuck right where they are. Now that you have done this work and are armed with these eternal truths, it is your opportunity to create anything you want.

The question posed in this chapter is, "Why does it matter?" It only matters if you want it to matter. If you are satisfied with what you are creating and how your life exists at this moment, you have already achieved your ultimate life.

Most people I talk to have deep and sometimes secret unfulfilled yearnings. Many relegate these desires to the world of impossible, with thoughts of "I'll never get that." If you live in that world, it will remain true for you until you leave this life or do something to change.

It matters because until you establish daily practices of intentional creation, most of what you do will fade away and be of little long-term benefit. God created us to sleep away about 1/3 of our lives. I don't know why. Next time I have a conversation with God, maybe I'll ask.

It seems as if we die every night and are reborn every morning. It is as if each day represents a new and vibrant opportunity for creation. Since that is the structure, embrace that reality with all your heart and furiously lean into the creation of each day like the precious gift it is.

Time and the choice of how you use it are the only things you have. Everything else is temporary and evaporates. Creating your life is a process that unfolds from moment to moment.

I use a morning ritual to intentionally create every day consistent with the principles declared in Part II and following the practices of "living in the present" and "loving what is." This allows the greatest access to infinite creative power.

Chapter 29

It's a Long Game

Creation and growth are a process. With rare exceptions, everything in the natural world grows and changes according to the laws of growth and the time it takes them to operate.

You don't go to the gym and go from a 100-pound bench press to a 500-pound bench press overnight. A tree doesn't grow from a seedling into a mature fruit-bearing wonder without some years in between. A baby is born helpless and completely dependent. Over time, the body and the mind grow and develop.

Bad soil and dry years cause tree rings to be spaced close together, representing minimal growth. Physical or mental challenges, troubled domestic situations, poverty or excessive wealth, and other externalities influence the development of every child.

The birth and development process of stars and planets is also a long-term process. Stable and predictable radioactive decay allows us to measure the age of things stretching into the distant past.

None of this is news. However, it makes me wonder why we have the expectation that everything we want should be done within the length of a TV sitcom. We expect to download and double-click to find the solution for every possible problem.

We expect instant wealth, instant fame, instant acknowledgment, or instant punishment for everything that happens. When that doesn't happen, we begin to blame, get frustrated, and think something is wrong. There is something wrong; it is with a flawed expectation.

As you conduct your journey of creating your life of purpose, prosperity, and joy, you will find both success and struggle. There will be things that go well, and situations that feel like a disaster. When you practice loving what is, you realize even in this growth process, you can choose joy.

Here is one example of choice. You can take the position your desired goal shouldn't take very long and become frustrated because it doesn't happen. Or you can embrace the truth, which takes as long as it takes, and enjoy the process. In fact, you can not only choose to enjoy the process, but realize the lengthy process is exactly what is required for your benefit.

Another powerful and rewarding choice is to only set goals that are in your control. A simple example is a person making money selling goods. They may have revenue targets, but they do not control the behavior of potential buyers. More meaningful goals are activity-based. Numbers of calls, numbers of conversations, length of time between follow-up contacts, and other things appropriate for the product.

Every organization has revenue targets, and the activity goals need to be adjusted based on observable results related to the revenue targets. Sales training, training in effective listening, deeper product knowledge, and other growth tools will also be applied.

Nearly all change is an iterative process. You are exactly as you are today. Learn to love yourself, without reservation, as you are in this moment. At the same time, identify things you want to be different. Learning to live in the present and learning to love what is, exactly as it is, are processes and not events.

Every piece of software goes through iterations. There is version 1.0, then 2.0, and so forth. Our personal growth efforts are exactly the same. I promise you will make multiple revisions of your declaration documents as you go through the process and as you experience life from your new point of view.

You know the view from a mountaintop is different than the view halfway up the slope. Just knowing that does not fully prepare you for the dramatic difference you experience from those two places. Your own understanding of your potential, the content and power of your declarations, and your ability to create life as you wish will also develop in a similar fashion.

When you see the results of your effort and the changes you make, the next steps will be obvious. Trying to fully map out the process from the beginning is like trying to understand the view from the top of the mountain before you start up the trail.

Settle in for the long game, commit to yourself, and then get moving. When you fall off the trail, skin your knee, or get your ego bruised, get up, get the bandages you need, and get back on the trail. The view from the top is worth it. That view can't be described well enough to let you experience it the same as you will when you get there.

Chapter 30

Morning What?

Everyone who has spent time in personal development has heard of a morning ritual. It is a trendy topic for books, courses, and pundits who alternatively praise and bash the need for and the benefits of such a process.

In creating my documents discussed in Part II, I realized implementation was key to getting any result. This is true for a couple of reasons. First, nothing happens until we start making changes. Second, experimenting with my declarations gave me insights I wouldn't get in any other way.

I'm not going to try to convince you to get up at 5 AM or some particular time to create your life. I choose to sidestep the whole conversation about morning people and night owls because it misses the point.

We live in a 24-hour world. Early in my career, I worked rotating shifts for 12 years. That required weekly adjustments of my sleep schedule and everything else. The key is recognizing one compelling truth. Whenever you sleep, that is your reset time.

After your sleep, you start your day, whatever the hour the clock says. If you want to have the best possible day, you need to prepare for that day. No athlete warms up after the game. No singer or instrumentalist warms up after the show. No account rep trying to close the big contract does final preparations for their presentation after the meeting.

Physical and mental preparation are absolutely essential for peak performance. When you compete with someone else, as in a sporting event, a musical contest, or in some business activities, the external measurements are set.

For most things in your life, measurements are yours to specify. I can't tell you how many times I hear people say, "I didn't get anything done today." Often, I ask, "What did you plan?" The answer is usually a vague statement of a few things they thought about. It is rarely a real plan of any consequence.

You are a thoroughbred. You are a champion racehorse. You are an infinitely valuable, infinitely capable, child of the divine. Your life is yours. You are the sovereign, and you decide the contents of every minute of every hour of every day.

Your choices unfold in the context of externalities that unfold around you. You can hate the externalities or love them. You can lean into whatever is around you, though you may be working to influence or change something in your world. Preparation of your spirit, your body, and your mind needs to happen before you engage in your joyful choice of creation.

That preparation is most effective at the start of your day when your mind is clear, your attention is not distracted, and you are most likely to have a focused and successful effort.

This daily work of preparation should include powerful reinforcement of personal truths you created in your Guiding Star documents. These are your own words and your own choices. They are not created to impress anyone or to check off some box about something you're supposed to be. This is the true, unvarnished, authentic you as you have declared yourself to be. If the statements aren't powerful and don't fire you up, do them again until they do.

As you learn and then master the ability to live in the present and love reality exactly as is, as you start each day, how you feel when you wake up, what you have scheduled, what your partner says or does, and other instant attention grabbers won't even matter.

If you are conscious, you are alive. Unless some immediate and overpowering physical distress dictates otherwise, you could choose to be flooded with gratitude at that first conscious breath. You can lay for a moment luxuriating in the truth that you have another day in front of you to mold as you will.

If you have a partner, you can express silent gratitude you have someone with whom you share your life, your creations, and your dreams. If the relationship is not powerful and productive at this time, you can acknowledge that truth and choose to love unconditionally anyway and be a gentle force for change.

Then, the words and meaning of your Guiding Star documents, your contract with eternity, enter your consciousness. You slowly repeat and marinate in the words you have chosen and the meaning you have created around those words.

If the words don't mean anything, that is a sign they need work. Nothing can alter the fact you are an infinite being with limitless potential. Nothing changes the truth; you create your existence, thought by thought, action by action, and moment by moment.

Sometimes people say to me, "I tried that morning ritual crap, and it doesn't work." Further questioning always reveals missing elements. Perhaps they are using a rote process without thinking. Perhaps the words were constructed from a video or an event they attended and are not truly their own. Perhaps they don't have their heart fully in the process.

The instructions in Part II will be just as useless if you create words that fail to light your soul on fire, statements that do not reflect your deepest desires, ideas to which you are only partially committed, or phrases you want to sound good or impress others.

There is absolute and eternal magic in creating the Guiding Star documents. It only occurs when you put your infinite magic and creativity into the process. It comes from you and your connection to the divine. If that connection is weak, the first order of business is to strengthen it.

Whatever time your day starts, your "morning ritual" is the key to success. Whatever effort is required to create this new habit is not only worth it but will soon reveal your daily preparation is something you never skip.

Chapter 31

SPEM

In this chapter, I describe my morning. It is how I create myself every day. You can model it if you like. To make it powerful for you, take your Guiding Star documents, however complete they may be, and ask yourself the following question: "What can I do in a daily preparation process that helps me be the person I have declared?"

As I answered that question, I created and refined a daily creation process using the acronym SPEM. This stands for Spiritual, Physical, Emotional, and Mental. I use these categories as a representation for all parts of my life.

I have seen models that divide life up into as many as 12 different areas. I find that too many for effective daily use. My definitions and process is described below.

Spiritual = all those parts of life concerning our relationship to larger forces. That being which resides inside of us which is not our bodies. Some expressions of this "larger-than-life" force are described here:

- Non-duality, or the feeling that we are all one.
- God, the organizing intelligence and intentional creator.
- The universe, or the set of realities that simply are.
- The three principles are divine mind, divine consciousness, and divine thought.

- Your higher self.
- The collective consciousness.

These aren't all the descriptions, just a few expressions to clarify the idea. The Spiritual category includes all these thoughts. I practice a specific spiritual tradition or religion, and honor and love every person's individual choice and effort to create their own relationship with the divine force.

The point is not to endorse a specific path or religious practice. Instead, it is to acknowledge the power and benefit of connecting to and regularly accessing what we all know to exist. Whether we pay much attention there or not, we have all experienced times when we know intuition guides us, we feel prompted to do certain things, and we turn heavenward for help.

This portion of the morning practice involves powerful connection, reinforcement, and recommitment to your Guiding Star documents created in Part II. Creating a set of documents with invincible statements will be useless unless it becomes part of the fabric of your life.

Intentional, focused, and rigorous recommitment to those principles is the most efficient and powerful way to weave them into your DNA and have them guide who you have chosen to become.

Physical = all aspects of the container of that spirit. Some describe it this way: "We are spiritual beings having a physical experience." We know the body is not the same as our consciousness.

Some people believe consciousness is not separate but is an outcome or consequence of physical processes in the body. My experience teaches otherwise. I know when we sit quietly and reflect on our own experience in life, we come to know there is a separate spiritual or energetic being.

The body is a separate entity from the spirit. Consider this: if you cut off an arm, the body is substantially changed, but the Spirit, though influenced, is still there and still watches and participates just as it did before the loss of the limb.

Some people lose both legs. Though confined to a wheelchair or other physical apparatus to assist with movement, the essence or being inside is the same. If you lost both arms, both legs and who knows what else, at what point do you actually affect the spirit, which is the essence of being?

There is no question the body holds the spirit, and must function to do so, but the essence seems to reside somewhere between the heart and the head. Regardless of the location of the spirit, the physical portion of the morning ritual centers on efforts to pay attention to and take care of the body.

Emotional = all the relationships we have fall in this section. I include my relationship with myself, my angel wife, and all the relationships with others. This area also includes all aspects of my emotional well-being and development.

This is a large group that encompasses:

- My relationship with myself.
- Romance with a partner.
- Friendships or various kinds.
- Caring for children.
- Caring for an aging parent or other family member.
- Colleagues at work.
- Friends at golf, tennis, or in other community activities.
- People at church.
- People you don't know yet.
- And many more.

I combine all the relationships not because they all feel the same. They don't. They are combined because all relationships come from feelings we have toward ourselves and others. Everything we feel comes from thoughts we believe and not from the other's thoughts, feelings, or actions.

The process of noticing, evaluating, and growing relationships of every kind is the same, regardless of the relationship. Paying attention to this critical area is essential for an effective daily creation process.

Mental = everything to do with developing and maintaining our mental capacity. This includes developing talents, upgrading knowledge, and everything else we need to stay mentally sharp and agile. For example, I play the piano. Keeping that skill alive and vibrant includes physical as well as mental work.

Studies repeatedly show the more we intentionally pay attention to our minds through study, analytical thinking, puzzles, skill development, learning new things, and every other effort, the more vibrant and capable we remain through many decades of life.

I intentionally sandwich every piece of life into one of these four areas. I do it to keep the number small enough to manage on a daily basis. You will build your morning process as you see fit so it fulfills every need you have for nourishment and development.

The Daily Practice – Connecting With Spirit

I put spiritual work first. It is the foundation for everything else. When our relationship with God or our higher power is vibrant and functional, the work in the other three areas is clearer, faster, and more effective.

My spiritual work always includes prayer. This is an intentional, focused conversation with God. I speak, and I listen. I receive answers in Revelation. I developed this skill with years of practice and cherish it above anything else. Intuition, inspiration, flashes of brilliance, and many other descriptions is how we describe this input from higher intelligence.

My spiritual work also includes sacred literature such as the Bible or other Scripture. It includes meditation, where I sit quietly or I walk or ride a bike in a setting that allows every other distraction to be eliminated and leaves me free to focus.

Learning to be with yourself in a way that allows you to have a quiet mind is a skill worth every effort. When I work with clients, I always start this process by helping them learn to meditate. Meditation is not complicated and doesn't involve strict discipline or rituals.

Meditation is three simple principles:

- Slow down enough to be where you are.
- Be still enough to notice what is there.
- Trust what comes to you is truth.

Slowing down is learning to stop moving your mind. It is simple enough to stop moving your body. Just sit down and don't move. If that is difficult, start with a short session and then do it for progressively longer periods of time.

If you walk or ride a bike to meditate, create the experience so there is very little jarring external input. You will learn to empty your mind of thoughts, allowing the recurring noise to simply drift off and focus on the here and now, as we discussed in Part I.

Being still is separate from slowing down. After you slow down and are fully present both physically and temporally, your mind begins to be quiet like undisturbed water. When that happens, you start to notice things you didn't notice before.

For example, if you sit quietly in a room and become fully present, you might notice the slight hum of an air conditioner or a bird through an open window. Those are things you would not have noticed without slowing down and being present.

Besides physical things, you will begin to notice other types of thoughts that come to you. They will feel different than the continuous flow of busyness and worry that typically flood your consciousness. To me, these thoughts seem a different color. Noticing these slower and quieter thoughts is what you practice.

The third step is simply a choice. When those different colored thoughts come, you can ignore them, you can treat them skeptically, or you can trust them. I have learned thoughts that come from this quiet and unhurried place contain messages and truth from God or your higher self.

Choosing to trust thoughts and feelings that come to you in this magnificent and relaxed stillness and peace is something you decide. I have chosen to trust that those sacred ideas that come in this space are from the divine. I have never been disappointed.

If you want help starting a meditation practice, consult *Meditation – The Amazing Journey Within.* This is the first of five volumes I wrote on meditation. They are available on Amazon. There are thousands of YouTube videos that demonstrate a variety of meditation practices. The point isn't the style. The point is to get started and maintain a regular practice, even though you might find it difficult or boring at first.

My daily meditation is so valuable, I never skip it for any reason. It creates time, gives powerful insights, and fuels the clarity and energy for my daily actions in a way that cannot be matched by any other practice.

During this meditation I repeat declarations from my documents. Sometimes, I go straight through, and other times, I stop and ponder deeply about one simple sentence. Inspiration always guides which idea needs loving and powerful focus today.

The Daily Practice – Honoring the Body

Honoring the body is essential for a powerful day. It creates your self-image and brings the focus and energy you need to create life exactly like you wish. When we don't feel good, everything is affected. Taking time to listen to and love the physical house of your spirit is the way to get there.

My physical activities are usually various forms of stretching and body-weight exercises. I practiced martial arts for decades, and have dozens of ways to wake up my body and honor all the joints, tendons and muscles. This process takes about 20 minutes. With many variations, it is never boring or repetitive.

Even if I intend to exercise more later in the day, this morning process to honor the body is non-negotiable. It moves your blood, moves your heart, and creates gratitude for life and breath.

Just as the spiritual practice energizes and enlivens the heart and spirit, honoring your body not only creates wakefulness and energy but also acknowledges the truth that the body requires separate attention and effort for maximum effectiveness.

The Daily Practice – Nurturing Relationships

One way to think about life is as an enormous web of relationships. You have a relationship with the universe or with the Spirit. You have a relationship with yourself. You have a relationship with those closest to you. You have relationships at different depths with everyone around you. Finally, you have a relationship with the entire world, including all those you don't know.

You can't accomplish anything alone. At least not anything of significance. Even if you were stranded on a desert island, your relationship with God and your relationship with yourself determine the quality of life you experience in that circumstance.

Intentionally taking time at the start of every day to consider and nurture relationships is a foundational exercise to support your mental and emotional health. It is also required to create Your Ultimate Life. Without this focused effort, you move through the day in a reactive fashion and will certainly miss things that need your attention.

My daily actions in this area flow from the spiritual work. During meditation, it is always true that names and ideas come to me. Those names are people I wish to nurture. I send text or voice messages in the morning to move that desire forward.

It might be a message of love, encouragement, acknowledgment, or other form of strengthening communication. It might be a repair attempt. If something has gone differently than expected or left a funny vibe in the world, I pay attention to those feelings. I send a message of apology, reconciliation, or invitation to start the dialogue or growth and reconciliation.

Next, I look through various social media threads and act on inspiration and ideas that come. Again, every effort is on creating, nurturing, or repairing some relationship. The work in the spiritual part of the ritual fuels this quite nicely. After meditation, I am filled with love and the desire for universal harmony.

The fruit that has come from these messages cannot be calculated. It is rarely fruitful in terms of direct business. It is always fruitful in terms of growth, building love, and doing things that, in our hearts, we know are the most important parts of life.

I might spend 10 or 15 minutes in this pursuit, or I might spend as long as an hour. It depends on the inspiration that comes about who to talk to, and the message to send. I find it a joyful and powerful time every single day. The beautiful part is I don't need anyone's permission or agreement to send love to those I choose.

The Daily Practice – Developing the Mind

Countless university and medical studies have demonstrated that regular time spent reading and learning is a huge factor in maintaining mental acuity, vibrant cognitive activity, and individual relevance in the rapidly changing world of today.

I find daily reading to be immensely enjoyable. I read a chapter or two across a wide range of topics every day. The result is that I read dozens of books a year and stay up to speed on many topics that I would never have thought about.

I find the more I learn, the more connected everything feels. Books on the origin of the universe, the relationship between matter and energy, discoveries of ancient civilizations, advances in chemistry and physics, studies about the effects of prayer on the mind, as well as innumerable books on personal development, are among the books I have read in the last year.

When I teach this practice to clients, I simply suggest starting with one chapter every day. The book can be about anything that interests you. I find nonfiction to be the most stimulating because it relates to the world as we know it and as we are discovering it.

The Daily Practice – Creating Your Own

I have shared my practices with you as an example. The important thing is to create your own. You will want to have many different ways to fill each of the categories you have in your morning routine.

Doing exactly the same thing every day can get tedious and lead to giving up. Develop at least five or six ways that fulfill each of the parts of life you choose to include in your preparation. Modify, adapt, change, and adjust as you go along. The important thing is to do it.

You can create all kinds of reasons not to.

- I don't have time.
- I don't see the point.
- It may work for others, but not for me.
- I tried that before, and it was stupid.
- It just doesn't work in my situation.
- And dozens of others.

Stop making excuses and get busy. It used to be difficult for me to maintain steady practice. It's normal to get confused and discouraged. Make a commitment to yourself and keep it. Get a good coach to help with both purpose and consistency.

I have maintained my morning ritual for so long that I would never start any day without it. It creates time, it creates power, it creates clarity, and it is the most effective thing I've ever done in turning the truths from my documents into my daily life.

The two most powerful and effective things I've ever done to change from who I was in 2007 to who I am today is, first, the creation and refining of my Guiding Star documents, and second, the creation, refinement, and constant use of a morning ritual that reinforces and cements the truth of those documents in my life.

I predict it will be the same for you.

Chapter 32

Start Where You Are

With all the conversation of powerful documents and rigorous practice, it might feel intimidating and almost hopeless in the beginning. It is not. It is available to you, here, now. No matter where you have been, you are where you are at this moment.

Your spiritual development is exactly where it is. Your physical attributes are what they are. The state of your relationships exist as they are in this moment. Your bank account is exactly as it is. Your habits around mental development exist in a certain state, right now.

There is absolutely nothing wrong with where you are at this moment. You are perfect, as you are, where you are, right now. People often talk about where they "should" be, what they "should" have, and what "should" have happened. That is arguing with reality and living on the resistance end of the continuum introduced in Chapter 9.

Every piece of your life is exactly where it is right this minute, and it is exactly where it "should" be because that's where it is. At the same time, you can be looking toward where you want to go from here. Living in the moment does not mean being unaware of what you are creating.

Starting where you are is the most obvious piece of advice. Yet, I am continually surprised at how often people try to start somewhere else. Some pretend they have more money than they do. Consequently, they live a lifestyle to maintain an image and get themselves in trouble.

Some might go to the gym and pretend they are stronger than they are and, therefore, get hurt. If I want to go to New York and I start in Denver, but pretend I am in Miami, I will drown somewhere out in the Bermuda Triangle.

Starting where you are is not an admission of failure or weakness. It is intelligent, important, and the very best place to start.

Using the four life areas from the morning ritual, you can take an assessment. Create your own measurements if the suggested ones don't speak to you. Where are you at this moment with respect to your Spiritual, Physical, Emotional, and Mental well-being?

I don't include money or finances in the SPEM framework because your ability to create value and, therefore, receive money is a natural consequence of focused attention on the four areas in the SPEM framework. The SPEM system is focused on daily preparation. When you are fully prepared and energized, you will maximize your productivity and value.

Creating value and money is an activity that takes place throughout the day on the days devoted to business. Depending on the situation and client I am coaching, I sometimes use the augmented acronym SPEM-B to include the business focus. Create your own method to include financial productivity and growth in your assessment.

The point of this chapter is two-fold. First, to help you start where you are without guilt, pretense or puffery. Second, to help you create an accurate assessment of the areas of life you choose to include in your daily focus and development. Accepting the truth of your present reality is an essential starting point. Arguing with reality brings all kinds of negative energy that will impede your progress.

Create the assessment so it makes sense for you. Don't get stuck on making it perfect or complete. Create it exactly as it occurs to you right now. Since it is yours and designed to serve and lift you, you can make changes as your experience dictates. You have ultimate freedom and sovereignty to create this process in the way that serves you best.

The main point is to tell the truth, assess with playful accuracy, and don't take anything so seriously it creates resistance. My experience shows working with a coach in this process is the most powerful way to complete this effort with greatest effect.

Starting where you are is intensely liberating. There is no need to pretend. There is no need to maintain a façade. There is the complete and absolute freedom of telling the truth, acknowledging to yourself exactly where you are, and then creating joyful declarations consistent with the truth of your divine nature and infinite possibility.

Declarations are always in the present tense and begin with "I AM" or a similar phrase. Using such declarative language has been repeatedly demonstrated to be the most powerful formulation.

If this is completely new for you, it may feel awkward at first. Do it anyway. The truth of your divinity is not in question. The truth of your infinite possibility is not in question. The only question is your belief about those truths.

Chapter 33

Starting Over

Everyone has seen a baby learn to walk. With varying degrees of parental encouragement and innate curiosity, the baby grabs an object and stands. Then he or she falls down with a thud. This process is repeated countless times.

At some point, the baby takes a step and then falls down with a thud. Undaunted, the baby tries again and again. Sometimes, there is frustration and tears. Sometimes, there is distraction, and the energy to learn evaporates.

Encouragement of parents, family members, and siblings keeps the attention focused and the will to try much higher. (That's one reason I love coaching as much as I do. My own experience being coached has had life-changing consequences in my growth.)

Eventually, and with enough thuds on a thickly diapered rear end, the baby learns to walk. Sometimes, the newly minted toddler resorts to familiar crawling because it seems easier at the moment. Regardless of the exact process, victory is achieved, and walking is mastered.

Quickly, the stumbles and tentative efforts evaporate, and the new achievement threshold is learning to run. Again, stumbles, bumps, and a few tears are the hallmarks of the process. At no point does the toddler or the family members who give encouragement ever think, "This walking stuff is too hard. I'll just crawl the rest of my life."

The comparison to this process is both humorous and obvious. Somewhere between learning to walk and creating our divine and infinite possibilities, we allow fear of failure, fear of others' opinions and judgment, and doubt in our own abilities to create powerful imaginary barriers.

I promise you right this minute, you will fall down a thousand times in the process of both creating your documents and living into the truth you boldly declare. That's a guarantee. The only question is how long you allow your bruised ego, the dents in your pride, and the tarnish of your reputation to keep you from moving forward.

There are three elements to the puzzle of the imaginary barriers. First is the opinions of others, or that which we believe others might be thinking. Second is internal judgment about where we ought to be. Third is our confidence in our divine nature's ability to grow.

Entire chapters and even books could be written about each of these. We will touch on them briefly, and I will share what I have learned from my own journey and from helping many others.

What others think of you is none of your business. First of all, you don't know what they think, and second, regardless of what they think, they have not lived your life, don't know your internal landscape, and are viewing life through their own lenses.

We live in a world where others' judgments about our worth, value, and status have real effects on jobs we get, promotions we receive, invitations we get, and many other things. You get to choose how much attention you pay to this. My advice is to pay zero attention.

Declaring your own guiding stars and living true to those declarations is the way to the greatest happiness, the biggest influence in the world, and creating the most prosperity. That is true 100% of the time. You can argue if you wish, but you will find, in the end, that stance is truth.

Our own judgments of where we ought to be, are wildly flawed. They usually come from external measurements and judgments that have been imposed on us and that we allow to define our beliefs on an ongoing basis.

Make your own declarations about who you are and where you want to be. Measure yourself against those declarations. Exercise extraordinary kindness and compassion as you fall repeatedly like a toddler. No one screams at a youngster as they learn to walk.

We look at the outstanding achievements of others and think we should already be where they are. We have no idea of the effort and work they expended behind the scenes to get where they are. Somehow, we think we should catapult to the top overnight. We then judge ourselves harshly because we're not done yet.

That view is harmful and creates significant self-inflicted pain. You are erecting barriers to your growth and blinders to your vision. Your declarations are agreements between you and God and need no permission or approval from others to be effective.

Our confidence in our abilities is dramatically affected by the real or imagined judgments of others and our own self-judgment. We often believe we are permanently barred from further achievement when we fail. We declare ourselves incapable or unable to get something done.

You can have anything you want. You can be anyone you want. You can do anything you want. You have infinite ability. You have divine support. Confidence is a choice and comes from repeated effort.

The only failure is giving up. When you fail or fall in any declaration, have self-compassion, love yourself more fully, clean up whatever mess you created, and recommit. You're guaranteed never to reach the top if you quit halfway up any mountain.

You have declared the truth of who you are just because you said so. If you achieve all your declarations in one go, they're not bold enough, and they certainly don't reflect your divine capability. I can also guarantee small declarations are not the kind that makes you weep every time you read them.

Since your declarations require no one's agreement and no one's permission, starting over when you fail or fall short is likewise a personal choice that requires nothing but your willingness to get up, fess up, clean it up, recommit, and joyfully move on with your creation process.

Chapter 34

Benefits in Love

We've talked a lot about how to make the declarations, how to implement a morning process to create yourself every day according to your personal truth, and how to move forward past the inevitable setbacks. All this takes real energy and focus. What is the payoff?

The benefits of this work can be measured. In this and the next few chapters, I describe the benefits I have seen in my life and in the lives of people I work with. I can't use words powerful enough to describe the scope of these benefits, but the language we have will have to do.

The difficulty of this dilemma can be described like this: "I can give you a menu to a fabulous restaurant. The offerings on the menu will list the contents and preparation of each dish. The review critics and other patrons can praise the flavor, texture, and preparation with incredible superlatives. None of that language even remotely prepares you for the truth that occurs when you take a bite."

Love is the creative force of the universe. It holds the worlds together, brings our consciousness into being, and is the gathering and nurturing force behind all things. It is the highest frequency, the brightest color, and the force that never fails.

It's easy to see this. We are attracted to love and light. We enjoy being in the presence of love, growth, unity, gathering, and community. We likewise see that hate, fear, anger, and the other feelings at the lower end of the spectrum are destructive. They separate, isolate, destroy, and decay.

Every powerful spiritual doctrine enshrines pure love as the central feature. The words of expression are different, but the central tenant is to love unconditionally, freely, unselfishly, and with the intent to serve and lift.

You already know this, but I say it anyway. Living in love for everyone all the time does not mean condoning negative action, ignoring injustice, or pretending away issues that need to be addressed. Here is a definition of love I find serves in nearly every circumstance.

Love is a verb. To think of love as a feeling is to dramatically limit the scope and power of this infinite force. As a verb, it requires action. To love someone is to make a choice to use your resources to serve and bless them.

To describe it in more detail, I use the same four areas as in my morning ritual. If I love someone, I use my Spiritual, Physical, Emotional, and Mental resources to lift them and bless them in their highest and best interest. The more of my resources I commit, the more love I express. To be most effective, it is required I do this with no thought of reward or personal gain.

You might think of all kinds of objections to or limitations in this definition. Choose not to argue with this definition for a moment. Instead, understand the intent and explore how it can encompass every kind of love. Romantic love, parental love, platonic love, brotherly and sisterly love, the love of the divine for each of us as His creations, and everything else.

As you choose to embrace your divine heritage, the love that already exists in the universe will infuse your soul with light and joy. As you choose to serve, the love you have will grow. Love is unique in that you cannot give it all away. The more you give, the more you are replenished by the infinite love in the universe.

Again, choose to understand I am not suggesting you neglect or destroy yourself or fail to take care of your body and your spirit in a false effort to "give away all your love." You can't draw water from an empty well. The entire process of daily creation is about filling your well to overflowing and maintaining a giant connection to the divine to continually replenish your supply.

When you realize how precious you are to the Divine, how much love went into creating you, and the scope of your infinite possibility, there is no need for concern about "getting your share" of whatever it is you're seeking.

I practiced the morning ritual and, in the process, refined my documents. The love I feel every moment of every day has grown so big I do not have language to describe it. Of course, life is full of twists and turns, unexpected events, and setbacks and situations I didn't expect, but I embrace them and find the gift in every glorious surprise.

Derivatives of this idea have shown up in self-help literature everywhere. "You can have anything in life you want if you just help enough other people get what they want." That is a paraphrase of a statement attributed to Zig Ziglar.

In the book *Influence,* Robert Cialdini teaches about the principle of reciprocity. We feel a desire to help those who have helped us. The Bible says we love God because he first loved us. That idea permeates all spiritual traditions and is reformulated and rephrased in every tradition of personal growth and system for impacting the world.

Creating and committing to powerful documents of your own choosing because they resonate with your soul is the starting point. Fearlessly and joyfully experimenting with how to make those documents the fabric of your daily life and every interaction will increase the love you feel and the power you have to add good to the world.

Chapter 35

Benefits in Time

Time is the one thing every single person has in equal amounts. Not that we live the same number of days, but that every day, for every person, there are 86,400 seconds. I'm ignoring relativistic time dilation and other mind-bending goodies.)

Even though everyone has the same amount of time, it certainly doesn't seem like it. Something I hear all the time is "I don't have enough time." I've come to realize I don't even know what that sentence means.

Each person who says that means something completely different. When I hear it, I dive into questions to understand the true meaning of the statement. Some common things we land on our these:

1. I have so many things other people expect me to do, I don't have time for things I want to do.
2. I don't make enough money, so I have to spend all my time working.
3. I have some health challenges, so I have no free time.
4. I have three little kids, so I have no time.
5. My spouse can't work, so I have to work two jobs to make ends meet.
6. Everybody else fills my calendar, so I have no time to myself.
7. I'm so busy the minute I sit down and relax, I fall asleep.
8. Fill in three or four of your own statements.

Regardless of your relationship with time, the fundamental truth is each of your days has 86,400 seconds. Another fundamental truth is we sleep somewhere between 25% and 33% of those seconds. How you fill the rest is up to you.

We only have two things in this world. We have time and the choice of what we do with it. What I learned is how I feel about my time affects both my perception of time and what I can accomplish with my allotment.

Interestingly enough, this is even true of the time I spend sleeping. My attitude about my time dramatically affects the quality and quantity of sleep I get and how refreshed I feel the next day.

The benefits from my documents and morning ritual related to time show up in three areas—awareness of time, productivity of time, and enjoyment of time. Remember, time passes at the same speed for every person.

Most people do not practice much in the way of awareness of time. Creating and refining the process of living fully in the present moment (8.64 seconds) helps me be aware of time as it passes. For this to be meaningful and effective, I eliminate all drama around the moments that pass.

I eliminate all negative energy like feelings of "I should be doing something else." Or thoughts like, "I'm wasting all this time." Those thoughts and the beliefs and feelings that follow create negative energy. This impedes creativity and eliminates enjoyment.

Take a moment now and think of any drama, guilt, questions, disturbance, and other upheaval you experience as time passes. Experience the full effect of this reflection. Is it positive or negative?

Awareness is not a hyper-focus or obsession with time. It is a calm awareness of using this resource. It is quiet, simple and clear. When you create personal declarations as contracts between you and the divine, and you create your life intentionally every day, you choose how you use time from a place of empowerment.

Of course, there are distractions. Of course, we fall. We make mistakes and take detours. That is why one of my declarations is "I AM that when I fall or fail in any of my declarations, I get up, fess up, clean it up, and recommit." Learning to make course corrections quickly and without internal drama saves a ton of time. It also makes course corrections fast and smooth.

You choose how much time you spend in productive action and how much time in refuel mode. When you cultivate your connection with the divine, you immediately feel at peace with your choice or prompted to make a change. This is a simple process. It is not easy, and it takes practice, but the rewards are staggering.

Productivity goes through the roof. Second-guessing disappears because you have your own personal document as your invincible guide. As you refine your document because experience teaches you or expands your view, the speed of reassessment and redeployment is nearly instantaneous.

When you eliminate worries about external judgment and focus on your own commitments to the divine, decisions become clear and fast. Dancing back and forth between multiple options, constant hesitation and overthinking evaporate.

Imagine that you could recapture all the time you spend second-guessing or criticizing yourself after a particular choice. For most people, that would be a generous amount. How much more productive would you be if you chose to live following only your personal set of commitments?

Most people I meet have a vague sense of what is right and, even so, adjust that standard regularly based on a situation and what is popular at the moment. This also happens when we include a list of things they "ought" to be doing and thinking in our definitions of "what is right."

Eliminate all "shoulds" and focus only on what you control. Your thoughts, your feelings, and your actions. In that context, choices are crystal clear, you live at peace in your heart, decisions are rapid and course corrections are natural and without fuss.

Enjoyment of your time is similarly enhanced. When you choose to live by a set of principles you commit to with all your heart, you stop worrying about what other people think. You are finally cured of the WITOT (What I Think Others Think) fungus. As you experiment with this process, you will be amazed at how pervasive that infection has been.

Even when your time is absorbed by activities you used to resent or demands from others you choose to accept, you can fully enjoy each of those moments because you choose to. Resentment is a choice; you can just as easily lean into and love the activity.

Practice this today. Every single thing you choose to do that previously created resentment, ask yourself "How can I love this activity?" Choose this while mowing the lawn, babysitting, or participating in something you previously committed to and now no longer want to do.

Your time is yours. Your time is your life. Your life is yours. Make a choice to love what you do. Build your awareness of each moment as it passes, make your documents real through daily practice, and choose to love everything you do. Your relationship with time will radically transform.

Chapter 36

Benefits in Purpose

I define the ultimate life as living in Purpose, Prosperity, and Joy by discovering, developing, and serving with skills I have developed, divine gifts, and life experience. Some people struggle with the term "Divine Gifts." Think of them as your natural abilities. Those things you seem skilled at and inclined toward to a greater degree than other people.

Every person who breathes air has these natural gifts. We often discount them because those things come easy to us, so we think they are of little worth. They are your most valuable assets. They are the first key to declaring purpose.

Your natural gifts may be obvious, like a gift in music, painting, writing, speaking, or some other visible expression. Other gifts are more subtle. The gift of listening. The gift of intuition. The gift of rapid learning, the gift of kindness, or the gift of just knowing what to do in a given situation.

You came here with these gifts. Perhaps you developed them in the place we were before. Perhaps they were gifts from your creator as you left the previous place and came here. They are clearly given to us to help both our enjoyment and success in this mortal experience.

When we die and leave this place to move on, those who love us and are still here often feel great sadness. I wonder if leaving our previous place and being born here was a celebration or equally sad. I suspect it was a celebration. After all, it included giving gifts. I also suspect if we truly understood how this grand plan is designed, leaving here to go onward would also be a celebration.

The next key to creating purpose in this existence is to look at those skills you have developed so far. These may be related to your natural gifts, or they may come from things you have chosen to do. Perhaps you went to school and studied accounting, aerospace engineering, or business.

Regardless of the area you studied, you developed a set of skills. Those skills are generally what you sell in the marketplace to create cash and make a living. Though you may be handsomely paid for some skill you developed in this fashion, it falls far short of your largest purpose and the greatest impact you can have in the world.

The third key is your life experience. As you go through life, you have thousands of experiences shaping your journey. How you interact with these experiences is always a choice and shapes everything you are.

As an infant, you are helpless and dependent on others' attention and care. Your actions and reactions are driven to get the attention and care you need to survive and grow.

Later, and that point in time differs for every person, you become aware that you choose how you interact with every experience. Many never learn this and go through life simply reacting to every situation and feeling frustrated at a lack of control. As we noted in Part I, we control very little of what happens around us. We control 100% of how we interact with those events.

These three keys, your natural gifts, your developed skills, and your life experience, weave a fabric of who you are. Each piece influences the others. Each piece strengthens and changes the others. Think of a braided nylon rope or a triple helix. Each of the three strands is a different color and represents one of these keys.

Your unique voice in the world is the combination of these three things. Woven together, this unique voice is the most powerful thing you have to express your true self, add good to the world, and make money by creating value. If you choose to use this voice fully and freely, you will have the most joy, make the largest impact, and make the most money.

Declaring a purpose for some period of your life or an overarching purpose for your entire life is a choice. This entire book is devoted to inviting you and helping you make such a choice and declare it with full and unwavering commitment.

Some events may trigger such a choice. However, in my observation, most people do not take the time to do the work of creating guiding stars as we did in Part II. Likewise, most do not consider these three keys and create a unique and powerful voice as they walk through the world.

Purpose is not something you find on your front porch delivered by Amazon. Purpose is a declaration you make because of the yearning of your divine soul to add good to the world, help those around you, and make a real difference.

Creating documents that represent your personal statements of commitment between you and the creator, in conjunction with exploring your natural gifts, developed skills, and life experience, will give you access to your unique voice and infinite creative power.

As a coach, nearly everyone I talk to, even casually, expresses a desire to "help other people." This yearning is part of the divine soul we brought with us from before. Exploring and developing that yearning is joyful for your soul and powerful for those you serve.

Finding your voice and declaring your purpose is iterative because our experiences and choices teach as we live. The processes we've explored together are the best ways I know to do this important work.

Your purpose will be a choice; it will evolve and expand over time. You will find and experience people and situations. People and experiences will find you. All these will add richness and texture to your life and your opportunities.

The key to awesome success is to make a firm declaration that you have a purpose, that you will find and declare it, or perhaps declare and then find it. The point is to get started, give in to the yearnings of your soul, and do the work required to create and own a purpose for your life.

Chapter 37

Benefits in Prosperity

We all need to eat, pay rent, handle bills, deal with emergencies, care for those who need us, have some recreation, and do other things as we move through life. From a very early age, we learn about work, money, and the need to be productive.

We also get contaminated with a bunch of stories about money. At least here in the Western world, we have turned money into a horrible religion. I say horrible not because money is horrible but because we have created a hierarchy, a set of judgments, class status, and other artifacts that cause pain.

This isn't a book or even a chapter about this religion or how to get untangled from that poisonous dogma. The fact is, we all need money to make life work. I use the word prosperity instead of money because prosperity is a much more expansive concept. Prosperity includes money and much more.

Money is an exchange medium that changes form and function. We used to trade goods we produced, then we developed exchange tokens, then we developed coins, then paper money, and now we just trade electrons in the cloud.

Money follows value, and so to create money, we need to create value. The money and value correlation isn't perfect because there is enormous value that never gets recognized or translated into cash. Even so, in the business world, if you create value or something people need, you can get paid.

For our purposes here, the question is, "How does living in the present and loving what is, creating my documents, making my declarations the foundation for my daily life, and finding my unique voice woven from the skills I have developed, my natural gifts, and my life experience, create value?"

The question might seem complicated, but it is amazingly simple. Right this minute, whatever job you have, you are selling a set of skills you developed. From delivering pizza to designing rockets to providing medical services to providing childcare, you are selling a service or a skill.

The first skill we develop and sell is rarely the best we have to offer. In a work setting, experience increases your value; you get promotions, learn shortcuts, create more value, and get paid more. That process still misses the largest contribution you have to offer.

Remember, you are a divine being with infinite potential. You came to this life with natural gifts. Divine gifts. These are things you do well with little thought or effort. Because they seem to come naturally and without much effort, you often don't realize their power or consider their worth.

Taking the time and effort to identify your natural gifts and learning how they can augment skills you have already developed is an opportunity to increase your value and make more money. If you make the effort, it is not difficult to see how that combination could serve you and those around you.

Your third value lever is your life experience or the things you have learned from the school of life. Choosing to consciously understand and integrate this experience is the gold. When you unconsciously go through life, reacting to things around you and living in resistance or acquiescence to reality, you are leaving most of your power on the table.

If you choose to love what is and allow every experience to refine you instead of creating resentment, your life experience begins to shape and strengthen the skills you develop and the natural gifts you already have. Then the magic happens.

Most of the time, people initially feel some fear about consciously and intentionally using life-shaping experiences to inform and direct how they show up in the world. People don't want to talk about their messes; they want to maintain a façade of success and fear what someone would think if the truth and the depth of personal struggle were known.

I'm not talking about just telling the story of struggle. I am talking about sharing the deep refinement that takes place when challenges become the crucible for divine connection, powerful choice, and exponential development.

Walking that road is simple but not easy. The path is not for the faint of heart. It requires honesty, commitment, and perseverance. But like climbing any steep mountain, the view from the top is fantastic.

Your most powerful contribution to the world, your opportunity for the greatest impact, and your road to prosperity and wealth come from doing the work, so your life experiences refine you and give you victory instead of victimhood.

When you combine the refinement provided by the rough road of life with the skills you develop and your natural gifts, you create a unique voice. I picture it as a three-part braided rope or a triple helix. This is the tool to satisfy your yearning to serve. It is the vehicle to create a real impact in the world, and it becomes the lever that allows you to make all the money you choose to accumulate.

I find in this process, the desire to get money for its own sake evaporates, and the wealth accumulated is constantly redirected into the growth of your impact, the love you can share, and your desire to serve and add good to the world.

Your membership in the cult of money worship is revoked, and the expansive definition of prosperity comes naturally into being. Your spiritual connections, your desire and ability to serve, the satisfaction deep in your soul, the richness of your relationships, and a glorious texture in the tapestry of your life flow almost effortlessly from your soul.

Chapter 38

Benefits in Joy

The ultimate life is a life of Purpose, Prosperity, and Joy created with choices in using our natural gifts, developed skills, and life experience to love, create, and serve while adding good to the world. That is my definition. I encourage you to create your own.

Joy is a lot bigger than fun. Joy is a lot bigger than happiness. Joy is the deepest, largest, and longest-lasting word we have to describe that sense of satisfaction, fulfillment, creation, and service. It includes the elements of love, compassion, forgiveness, and all the rest of the power words.

Joy is a choice. It is also a byproduct and outcome of other choices. If you choose a life of service and focus your spiritual, physical, emotional, and mental resources on blessing the lives of others, you will experience joy.

It comes without seeking it. It comes in unexpected and unpredictable ways. It floods your soul like warm sunshine on a summer day. It comes when you know, without a doubt, you are doing the things you are called to do in this world.

Sometimes, you might wonder, "How do I know what I am called to do in this world?" If you learn to live in the present moment, learn to love what is, and seek the inspiration from the divine sources greater than yourself, you will come to know.

Learning to listen to intuition is a powerful skill. Cultivating internal peace so there is nothing blocking your access to intuition is another powerful skill. Choosing to act on intuition without fear or delay is a powerful mastery of living a guided life.

Speaking these words may seem impossible or arrogant. It is not so. God, your creator, has in mind that you experience every possible joy. Discarding a weak definition of joy, which might be "that everything goes fluidly and without too much trouble," is key to a rich and textured life.

We are built to love and serve each other. We experience the greatest sense of internal satisfaction and completeness when we are in love and service. We live in a world that focuses on self-gratification and "me first." That often causes the still, small voice of the Spirit to be drowned out in the cacophony of daily existence.

Living in the present moment, choosing to love what is, declaring your own commitments to the divine, and living those commitments to the best of your ability every day while cleaning up whatever messes we create is the path to unbelievable joy.

The foundation and application of this entire process is very simple but not easy. Choose love over fear every time. Choose finding opportunity over helpless victimhood every time. Create declarations between yourself and God that connect you to who you are, and use them daily. Clean up whatever messes you make, not because you're supposed to, not because you got caught, not because you're embarrassed, but because it is who you have declared yourself to be.

This is a journey that begins the moment you decide it begins.

Joy is the natural outcome of every choice that honors your divine nature, natural gifts, and personal commitments. Joy is the natural outcome every time you make a choice to love and serve.

Following this path will create joy you have not yet imagined.

Chapter 39

The Ultimate Life

No matter how you were raised, socialized, and taught. No matter what your life experience has inflicted on you up to now. No matter what circumstance and society cram down your throat as "the cool thing" to do, to have, or to be. You are the sovereign of your life.

In 2007, I was making enough money, so my $3000 a week cocaine habit didn't matter. I was at the pinnacle of a career with important positions and decision-making authority that affected billions of dollars. I was also miserable.

My heart was empty, I had no purpose, and I flooded my life with distractions so I could have temporary relief from the pain that was my hourly companion. I attempted suicide twice. The divine intervention in August and September 2007 offered an invitation to explore something new.

Without having any idea where the road would lead, and without having any idea how to do what I set out to do, I walked away from everything I had built and started over.

The journey has been rough; the path has been rocky, mistakes have been plentiful, learnings have been overflowing, and the need to clean up messes has been endless.

The change has been astounding. The new direction gets clearer and more attractive with every passing moment. Misery is a distant memory. My connection with the divine grows stronger with every passing breath. I have absolute clarity and certainty about my purpose, my daily actions, and everything I am doing.

I know who I am and what I am about. This book is an invitation for you to take the same journey.

If I can go from a broken, suicidal, addicted, pretentious, fearful, self-sabotaging, arrogant, duplicitous, vacuous, terrified person with no clue about how to change, where to start, how to fix anything, and no idea what the future holds to where I am today, you can too.

Today, as I write this, my commitment this year (my year goes from October 14, 2023, to October 14, 2024) is to help 250 million people discover the truth of who they really are and create from that infinite possibility.

It's the only thing I do each day and every day. All the books I write, all the music I compose and sing, all the talks I give, all the podcasts I produce, and all the speeches I give are aimed at this objective.

I have come to realize I need nothing. I am complete and full at this moment. My glorious and beautiful companion, who is aptly named Joy, is with me every step of this path and is just as committed to the outcome as I am.

Today, I live the ultimate life by every definition I have. I cannot tell you how to define your ultimate life. I know without question it is possible for you to declare it and achieve it. I also know nothing will happen if you don't start where you are and make intentional and bold choices to move forward and begin your own creation.

The details of the dramatic changes that began in August 2007 and all the work that followed are contained in *Tightrope of Depression* and *Down From the Gallows.* The third and final volume of that trilogy will be published in early 2025.

The purpose of this book is to give you everything I can possibly give you about the powerful things that helped me along the way. First is learning to live in the present moment (8.64 seconds.) Second is learning to love what is. Embrace it and create from your present moment and your present reality.

Third is the set of declarations that are your personal contract with God. They are yours to define, yours to adjust and make powerful, and yours to cherish. Fourth is a daily commitment to a morning preparation process so that everything I have declared becomes the visceral, palpable, tangible, guiding truth that moves me through each moment.

As I write this, I am 16 years on from the start. In that time, I have walked the path, bled on the floor, died in the hospital, and had many other experiences that could have pulled me away. Each one is a blessing and a refinement of my soul.

There is nothing special about me. I have no superpowers which are not available to you. I have no connection with God, which is not available to you. I have no access to things you can't have. This book is an invitation for you to make a choice and begin your own road to creating your ultimate life.

Chapter 40

Stay the Course

No matter how often I repeat the truth, "I have nothing that you can't have," people don't believe me. Perhaps you doubt your own ability to create the things you want, as I have created mine. I know exactly how that feels.

In 2012, I had an experience that may surprise you. 2012 was five years after I began this journey. I had already spent countless hours with therapists and in deep work creating myself as a new person. I had just begun to realize I felt called to be a coach, or to be in the "people encouragement" business.

I attended a full-day event put on by one of the most notable speakers on the planet. The purpose of the event was to teach how to use personal story to create a message and business. Of course, at the end of the event, there was an upsell to a three-day Boot Camp to master the art of storytelling.

I was already an experienced speaker. During my executive work, I spoke at dozens of conferences around the world. I appeared at universities as a guest lecturer, and I had a reputation as a fabulous presenter. I had also successfully run hundreds of stakeholder meetings with vocal and sometimes unruly participants.

Right at the end of the talk, when he was completing the sales pitch, a feeling of frustration and hopelessness welled up in my heart. It spilled into my eyes, and I wept tears of frustration. I got up and stomped out of the conference.

The talk was fabulous. The story was astounding; his presentation was the best I had ever seen. I knew I had speaking chops that were as good or nearly as good as his. So what in the world was causing this frustration?

As I left the room, I muttered under my breath and through the tears, "I could do this too if I only had a story like his. But me, I got nothin'!" I meant that with all sincerity.

When I tell this to clients today, they roll their eyes and laugh in amazement. This is book number nineteen, and I have several more underway. I have spoken at hundreds of seminars on personal development, incredible transformation, and personal power. I have at least a dozen keynote speeches I can give right now.

All the books, all the products, all the lectures, and all the opportunities I have today come from the stories right out of my life. It wasn't that I didn't have a powerful and amazing story. I did, and I do. I just didn't know it.

You have the same power.

While reading this book, you may feel like "I got nothin'," just like I felt. I guarantee you, with 100% certainty, that you have limitless power, infinite opportunity, and an awesome life story right this minute, right where you are.

Like me, you may not know what you have.

I discovered the gold in my life and my story as I walked the path of creating my life exactly as I have described in this book. Creating a relationship with God. Exploring and declaring a purpose for my existence. Digging into and reconciling with my thorny and fiery history. Taking responsibility for my past, present, and future. It's all there; you just have to go get it.

Fully 75% of people I work with begin the journey convinced they have nothing important to offer, their voice isn't powerful, and they can't really make a difference in any significant way.

You won't know what you have until you get on the journey. Put away all the stories about who you used to be and invite all the voices who tell you what you aren't to leave the stage and even the auditorium. They no longer control your world.

You are a child of God. Nothing you can do or say will change that truth. You were given natural gifts as you came to this world. You have developed a set of skills that have allowed you to make money and survive up to this moment. You have a unique and powerful life experience that gives you a voice and perspective different from anyone else's.

If you take your existing skills, natural gifts, and your life experience, you can create declarations that thrill your soul, inspire your action moment to moment, and act as a guiding star for every day you breathe and every goal you aspire to.

You will be discouraged. You will fall short. You will want to quit. So did every person who ever walked this path. Your choices are simple and clear. You can start or not start. You can continue or not continue. That is the same choice in each moment of your life.

Speak boldly. Create an amazing vision and let nothing get in your way. Rest when you must, but never stop moving forward with intention and power.

Stay the course!

Chapter 41

Getting Help

If I think about the attitudes, decisions, and actions that helped me partner with the Divine, create a miraculous transformation, and live the ultimate life I now enjoy, it is easy to make a list. The list is endless because growth is a mountain without a top. I also find it fun. This list is not necessarily in order and it is certainly not complete.

- Make a final decision I was going to change.
- Figure out where I needed help.
- Stop lying to myself.
- Write a beginning description of what that change looks like.
- Figure out the smallest steps I could take to get started.
- Learn to forgive myself.
- Learn to love myself.
- Look for ways to love and serve others.
- Stop worrying about what anyone else is thinking.
- Choose to be vulnerable about my mistakes, learnings, and growth.
- Forgive everyone and everything all the time (this is essential or I can't forgive myself.)
- Revise the description of my desired changes, again and again.
- Create documents that reflect my firm commitments.
- Create a daily ritual that reinforces my commitments.
- Relentlessly implement the daily ritual that reinforces my commitments.

- Regularly explore areas I fall short.
- Revise the daily ritual that reinforces my commitments.
- Drop the drama of judging myself and others.
- Lean into the truth that growth is a process and mistakes are inevitable.
- Create a definition of love.
- Live my definition of love.
- Choose to love everything exactly as it is.
- Look for more ways to love and serve others.
- Write books about all of the things I discover.
- Write songs about all of the things I discover.
- Learn to meditate powerfully and regularly.
- Revise this list over and over.
- Find more ways to serve every person I meet.
- Refine my declarations about my life direction.
- Apologize for mistakes the instant I make them.
- Fix the mistakes I make to the best of my ability.
- Love my wife more.
- Love myself more.
- Serve my wife with every breath.
- Remember to love my wife more.
- Express gratitude at least 50 times a day.
- And the list goes on.
- Start at the top and do all of it all over again.

This might sound like a silly list and an impossible task. Growth is a mountain with no top. It is also a joyful journey with its own reward. Every new view of the universe and of myself is invigorating, inviting and so full of joy.

There is no way any human breathing air can do this work on their own.

One of the most important and powerful things I did in this journey was to get help. One glaring characteristic of my previously broken life full of depression, addictions, self-sabotage, and isolation, was I refused to get help. I was ashamed of my failings. I was embarrassed at my seeming ineptitude. I believed everything was my fault and I needed to fix it alone.

Not only is that impossible, it is also not the design of our existence. We are built to love and serve each other. Seeking and accepting help is a sign of strength, not weakness. It is a sign of maturity and growth, not failure.

The help I sought came from God, counselors, my companion Joy, and numerous coaches. When I started on the journey to becoming a coach, I had absolutely no idea how rewarding the profession was and how much I could benefit from being coached.

Whatever the reason, I had no experience with receiving coaching in my entire life before the dramatic change in 2007 that I described in *Tightrope of Depression.* Now, I can't imagine not having a powerful coach in my corner who is dedicated to my growth and expansion.

No top performer in any field, business, music, art, acting, leadership, or anything else, got there without help. I think of coaching as the "people encouragement" business. It is glorious, rewarding, and has a fabulous impact on both the coach and the clients.

Do not hesitate. Go get the help you need. Boldly declare your commitment and begin your journey with joy, excitement, and determination. Get the help you need, and get started.

The information is in the appendix if you want information about tools, courses, books, and programs I offer. I would love to know you, help you, and participate in your own glorious growth and transformation.

Epilogue

We are getting ready to move from Edmonton, Alberta, to Vancouver Island. We decided on this about 18 months ago and set the date for the end of summer 2022. The months came and went, and it was clear we weren't ready.

We reset the clock and decided to move at the end of summer 2023. There was no drama and no sense of failure or disappointment. It just became clear the timing wasn't right yet.

I am writing this book in the summer of 2023. We just reset the clock again and decided to move at the end of summer 2024.

Again, no drama. We have embraced what is and chosen to love it with all our hearts. That said, we really want to get out of the fierce winters that are part of living in Edmonton. It will be one more adventure that adds richness and texture to life.

This path of living life completely embracing what is while joyfully planning for miracles and magic has become the norm. Joy and I live the ultimate life of purpose, prosperity, and joy every week, every day, and every moment.

Love is the fuel, love is the reward, and creation and fun permeate every moment. As we reset the goals, we considered what we would complete between now and the move next summer.

I am fully engulfed in my commitment this year to help 250 million people discover who they really are, choose to create from their infinite possibilities and serve with their divine gifts and life experiences. Nothing could be more wonderful or fulfilling.

The life I left 16 years ago is a distant memory. At the same time it remains powerful evidence of the scope and possibility of change and growth available to every person who breathes air. This includes you.

I invite you to let this book change your life. Take each principle and ask yourself the important questions that run through your mind as you read the stories. Read them all about you, even though I am the actor. There is nothing special about me. You are divine and have infinite opportunity.

Ask yourself the following questions and then dig in deeply to find and create answers.

- Who do I need to be to create more love in my life?
- Who do I need to be to love myself fiercely and deeply?
- Who do I need to be to forgive everyone and everything?
- Who do I need to be to discover and trust in my divine nature and gifts?
- Who do I need to be to serve those around me fiercely and lovingly?
- Who do I need to be to create and declare a life purpose?
- Who do I need to be to create all the prosperity I ever dreamed of?
- Who do I need to be to love my partner more?
- Who do I need to be so every moment of life is a joy?
- Who do I need to be to start this journey right now?
- Who do I need to be to stay on the path forever?
- Who do I need to be to get up, fess up, and clean it up, whenever I fail?
- Who do I need to be to make myself exactly as I dream?
- Who do I need to be to find the help I need?
- Who do I need to be to believe I am worth every effort?

- Who do I need to be to see each person in their divine capability?
- Who do I need to be to live in love and service?

Add to this list every question that makes sense to you.

After asking the questions that call to you, make the needed investment of time, self-examination, getting help, and creating change to find and live the answers that light your soul on fire. Then start over and do it again.

I love you.

Appendix

Resources and Contact Information

In my work as a coach, I am focused on helping people do things they don't believe they can do. That involves overcoming all the opposing forces that convince us we are less than capable.

I have a lot of free resources available, including my podcast: Your Ultimate Life Podcast with Kellan Fluckiger, available on all of the popular podcast platforms. You can subscribe or listen to an episode here, https://www.yourultimatelifepodcast.com

I upload new videos twice weekly on my YouTube Channel: Ultimate Life Formula. The URL is https://www.youtube.com/c/UltimateLifeFormula.

Below is a list of all the resources referred to in this book and information about where to access them. All the books are available on Amazon, from the publisher or directly from me. They're listed below.

Also included is contact information if you want to contact the author the publisher, or have further discussions about your book, or inquire about coaching.

- Walking Without Fear
- The Results Equation
- Meeting God at the Door
- The Tightrope of Depression
- The Book of Context
- Meditation, The Amazing Journey Within, Volume I-V
- The Story Arc

- In addition, I conduct regular workshops on topics like:
    - The Story Arc™
    - Time Creation – Systems to Multiply Productivity
    - Ultimate Life Transformation Experience (www.ultimatelife.ca)
    - Live Without Fear (www.livewithoutfear.ca)
    - Creating Energy – Systems for Limitless Power
    - Coaches – Learn to Crush Your Client Enrollment (www.ultimatecoachingformula.com) AND our popular challenge for coaches, www.lovecoachsignem.com
    - Learn to Meditate – guided meditation audio and video (available on my website, www.kellanfluckiger.com)

I also conduct 6-month goal achievement workshops called *The Results Equation Intensive.* These are designed to help you accomplish a major goal in six months or less. They are held "virtually" and can be attended from anywhere.

I have other kinds of coaching arrangements to help people with any situation where they are finally committed to ending their addiction to mediocrity and creating the life of their dreams.

Contact information is below, and I welcome the opportunity to get to know you.

For Kellan's latest shows, you can find him On Demand and Network TV (Traverse TV) at https://watch.traversetv.com/browse/

Video is amazing, and you'll find lots of free resources, including how you can create and live your ultimate using your existing skills, life experience and natural gifts and talents at www.yourultimatelife.ca.

Websites: www.KellanFluckiger.com and if you are a coach and are having trouble filling your coaching practice, visit www.lovecoachsignem.com to learn more about our 5-day challenges.

Contact the Publisher at: RedAussiePublishing@gmail.com

Connect with me through Facebook at https://www.facebook.com/kellan.fluckiger3 and Pinterest at: https://www.pinterest.com/coachkellan/

About the Author

Kellan Fluckiger is the author of the #1 best-selling books Tightrope of Depression, The Results Equation, Forgiveness, The Book of Context, Meeting God at the Door, Meditation, The Amazing Journey Within, Walking Without Fear, and The Story Arc.

He is an in-demand speaker and a highly successful coach. Working with CEOs of companies large and small, Kellan has touched and transformed many lives over the past 30 years.

A certified master coach and former C-suite Executive, Kellan has coached everyone from Super Bowl winners to BMI music award winners and everyone in between.

Kellan is a master at high achievement. As a motivational speaker and business coach, his journey has benefited thousands.

Kellan runs several small group coaching programs, six months in length. This personal transformation intensive is for leaders and visionaries who want to end addiction to mediocrity, shed old baggage, eliminate old stories, drop old grudges, and fully unleash their creativity and power to achieve amazing gains in productivity, prosperity, and personal fulfillment.

In addition to coaching, Kellan has written, recorded, and produced 11 albums of original music. He's been running a successful recording studio for over 35 years.

Kellan is a master of creation and has created an engaging and entertaining podcast, Your Ultimate Life, which is available on all popular podcast networks, along with a weekly show on LA Talk Radio. In addition to his podcast, Kellan is busy creating programs and courses to support creatives, entrepreneurs, and leaders on their journey through struggles and victories as they discover, develop, and deliver their talents to the world.

For the most up-to-date information on Kellan's creations, visit his website at www.kellanfluckiger.com or www.yourultimatelife.ca.

Born in San Francisco, CA, Kellan now spends most of the year creating and writing in Canada with his wife, Joy, their two cats and dogs, and with extended family.

Made in the USA
Las Vegas, NV
29 March 2025

20265935R00121